GOD the Bible and YOU

GOD the Bible and YOU

R. A. Torrey

Whitaker House

GOD, THE BIBLE, AND YOU

ISBN: 0-88368-581-7
Printed in the United States of America
Copyright © 1999 by Whitaker House

Whitaker House
30 Hunt Valley Circle
New Kensington, PA 15068

Library of Congress Cataloging-in-Publication Data

Torrey, R. A. (Reuben Archer), 1856–1928.
    God, the Bible, and you / by R. A. Torrey.
       p.   cm.
    Includes bibliographical references.
    ISBN 0-88368-581-7 (pbk.)
    1. God—Biblical teaching. I. Title.
BS544.T67 1999
231—dc21   99-15911

1 2 3 4 5 6 7 8 9 10 11 12 13 /11 10 09 08 07 06 05 04 03 02 01 00 99

Contents

1. Is the Bible Inspired by God? 7

2. Who Is the God of the Bible? 31

3. Is God Perfect, and Is He One? 51

4. Is Jesus Christ God? 71

5. Is Jesus Christ Truly Man? 93

6. Is the Holy Spirit a Person? 115

7. Is the Holy Spirit God, and Is He Separate
   from the Father and Son? 147

Is the Bible
Inspired by God?

1

Is the Bible Inspired by God?

*For prophecy never came by the will of man,
but holy men of God spoke as they were
moved by the Holy Spirit.*
—2 Peter 1:21

*All Scripture is given by inspiration of God,
and is profitable for doctrine, for reproof, for
correction, for instruction in righteousness, that the
man of God may be complete, thoroughly
equipped for every good work.*
—2 Timothy 3:16–17

To what extent is the Bible inspired by God? The answer to this question is of vital and fundamental importance. We must understand that the writers of the various books of the Bible were inspired by God in a sense that no other men were ever inspired by God. Indeed, they were so gifted and taught and led by the Holy Spirit in recording the words of the Bible that they taught the truth and nothing but the truth. Their teachings were absolutely without error. We have in the Bible a court of final appeal and of infallible wisdom to which we can go to settle every question of doctrine or duty.

However, many believe that the writers of the Bible were "inspired" only in the vague and uncertain sense that Shakespeare, Browning, and many other men of genius were inspired. In other words, they were inspired only to the extent that their minds were made more keen to see the truth than ordinary men, and they still made mistakes and chose the wrong words to express their thoughts. Those who believe this false but popular doctrine say that we must recast the Bible writers' thoughts by discovering, if we may, the inspired thoughts behind the uninspired words.

If this is the case, we are all lost at sea. We are in hopeless confusion, for each generation must then settle for itself what the Holy Spirit meant to say through the blundering Bible writers. However, since no generation can determine with any accuracy what the Spirit meant, no generation can arrive at the truth but must simply promote blunders for the next and wiser generation to correct, to be corrected in turn by the next generation. Thank God that this subtle doctrine can be proven to be utterly untrue!

There is a great need for crystal clear teaching on this subject. Our seminaries, pulpits, and Sunday schools, as well as our religious literature, are full of teaching that is vague, inaccurate, misleading, unscriptural, and often grossly false. Many people these days say, "I believe that the Bible is inspired," when by "inspired" they do not mean at all what we understand or what the mighty men of faith in the past meant by inspired. They often say that they "believe the Bible is the Word of God," when at the same time they believe it is full of errors.

But the Bible is as clear as crystal in its teachings and claims regarding itself. Either those claims are true, or the Bible is the biggest fraud in all the literature of the human race. The position held by so many today—that the Bible is a good book, perhaps the best book in the world, but at the same time is full of errors that must be corrected by the higher wisdom of our day—is utterly illogical and absolutely ridiculous. If the Bible is not what it claims to be, it is a fraud—an outrageous fraud.

What does the Bible teach and claim concerning itself? What does it teach and claim regarding the fact and extent of its own inspiration?

PREVIOUSLY UNDISCOVERED TRUTH WAS REVEALED

The first thing taught in the Bible regarding the inspiration of the various authors of the books of the Bible is this: truth hidden from men for ages, which they had not discovered and could not have discovered by the unaided processes of human reasoning, was revealed to the Bible writers by the Holy Spirit. We find this very clearly taught in the Word of God:

> *If indeed you have heard of the dispensation of the grace of God which was given to me for you, how that by revelation He made known to me the mystery (as I have briefly written already, by which, when you read, you may*

understand my knowledge in the mystery of Christ), which in other ages was not made known to the sons of men, as it has now been revealed by the Spirit to His holy apostles and prophets. (Eph. 3:2–5)

The meaning of these words is unmistakable. Here Paul declared very plainly that God *"by the Spirit"* had revealed *"to His holy apostles and prophets"* *"the mystery of Christ."* This mystery had not been made known to the sons of men in former generations. Men had not discovered it and could not discover it, except by revelation from God. But Paul and the other apostles and prophets knew it by direct revelation from God Himself through the Holy Spirit.

The Bible contains truth that men never had discovered and never could have discovered if left to themselves. The Father, in great grace, has revealed this truth to His children through His servants, the prophets and apostles. This teaching is inescapable.

We see the foolishness, a foolishness so common in our day, of seeking to test the statements of Scripture by the conclusions of human reasoning. The revelation of God transcends human reasoning; therefore, human reasoning cannot be its test. Furthermore, Christian reasoning is the *product* of studying the truth of the Bible; it is not the *test* of the truth of the Bible. If our reasoning differs from the statements of the Bible, the thing for us to do is not to try to pull God's revelation down to the level of our reasoning, but to elevate our reasoning to the level of God's Word.

THE REVELATION TO THE PROPHET WAS INDEPENDENT OF HIS OWN THINKING

A second thing about the inspiration of the Bible writers that the Bible makes perfectly clear is this: the revelation made by God through His Holy Spirit to the prophets was independent of the prophets' own thinking. It was made to them by the Spirit of Christ, who was in them. They themselves often did not thoroughly understand the full meaning of what the Spirit was saying through them. In fact, they diligently searched and inquired in their own minds as to the meaning of what they themselves had said. This point comes out very plainly in 1 Peter:

> *Of this salvation the prophets have inquired and searched carefully, who prophesied of the grace that would come to you, searching what, or what manner of time, the Spirit of Christ who was in them was indicating when He testified beforehand the sufferings of Christ and the glories that would follow. To them it was revealed that, not to themselves, but to us they were ministering the things which now have been reported to you through those who have preached the gospel to you by the Holy Spirit sent from heaven; things which angels desire to look into.* (1 Pet. 1:10–12)

Here, again, the meaning is clear; it is inescapable. We are told that the prophets had a revelation made to them by the Holy Spirit, the meaning of which they did not thoroughly comprehend. They themselves *"inquired and searched carefully"* as to the meaning of this revelation that they had received and recorded. Through them the Spirit testified beforehand about *"the sufferings of Christ and the glories that would follow."* (See, for example, Isaiah 53:3 and Psalm 22.) They recorded what the Spirit testified, but what it meant they did not thoroughly understand.

It was not merely that their minds were made keen to see things that they would not otherwise see and they therefore more or less accurately recorded them. No, there was a very definite revelation, arising not from their own minds at all, but from the Spirit of God. This they recorded. The revelation was not of themselves, for they themselves wondered about its meaning. What they recorded was not at all their own thoughts; it was the thoughts of the Holy Spirit who spoke through them. How utterly different this concept is from what is so persistently taught in many of our pulpits and theological seminaries!

PROPHETIC UTTERANCES WERE FROM GOD HIMSELF

The third thing that the Bible makes perfectly clear is that not one single prophetic utterance was of the prophet's own will (that is, it was not in any sense merely what he wished to say). In every instance, the prophet's words were from God, and the prophet was "carried along" in the prophetic utterance by the Holy Spirit, regardless of his own will or thoughts. We find this stated in so many words in 2 Peter 1:21, where we read,

> *For prophecy never* [literally, "not a prophecy ever"] *came* [literally, "was brought"] *by the will of man, but holy men of God spoke as they were moved* [literally, "carried along" or "borne"] *by the Holy Spirit.*

There can be no honest mistaking of the meaning of this language. The prophet never thought that there was something that needed to be said and therefore said it, but God took possession of the prophet and *carried him along* in his utterance by the power of the Holy Spirit. The prophet did not speak by his own reasoning or by his own intuition; he spoke *"by the Holy Spirit."* As God's messenger, he spoke what God told him to say.

THE HOLY SPIRIT WAS THE REAL SPEAKER

The fourth thing that the Bible teaches regarding the inspiration of the Bible writers and their utterances is that the Holy Spirit was the real speaker in the prophetic utterances. What was said or written was the Holy Spirit's words, not the words of the prophet. This truth is revealed repeatedly in various Scriptures.

For example, in Hebrews 3:7–8, we read, *"Therefore, as the Holy Spirit says: 'Today, if you will hear His voice, do not harden your hearts.'"* The author of the epistle to the Hebrews was quoting Psalm 95:7–8; he said that what the psalmist is

15

recorded as saying is actually what *"the Holy Spirit says."*

Again, in Hebrews 10:15–16, we read,

> *The Holy Spirit also witnesses to us; for...He had said before, "This is the covenant that I will make with them after those days, says the* LORD: *I will put My laws into their hearts, and in their minds I will write them."*

Now, the author of the epistle to the Hebrews is quoting Jeremiah 31:33, and he does not hesitate to say that the testimony that Jeremiah gave is *the testimony of the Holy Spirit,* that the Holy Spirit was the real speaker.

We read in Acts 28:25–27 that Paul said,

> *The Holy Spirit spoke rightly through Isaiah the prophet to our fathers, saying, "Go to this people and say: 'Hearing you will hear, and shall not understand; and seeing you will see, and not perceive. For the hearts of this people have grown dull. Their ears are hard of hearing, and their eyes they have closed, lest they should see with their eyes and hear with their ears, lest they should understand with their hearts and turn, so that I should heal them.'"*

Here Paul was quoting Isaiah's words as recorded in Isaiah 6:9–10, and he distinctly said that the real speaker was not Isaiah, but *"the Holy Spirit"* who spoke *"through Isaiah the prophet."*

Turning now to the Old Testament, we read in 2 Samuel 23:2 this assertion by David regarding the things that he said and wrote: *"The Spirit of the LORD spoke by me, and His word was on my tongue."* There can be no mistaking the meaning of these words on the part of anyone who goes to the Bible to find out what it really claims and teaches. The Holy Spirit was the real speaker in the prophetic utterances. It was the Holy Spirit's utterance that was upon the prophet's tongue. The prophet was simply the mouth by which the Holy Spirit spoke. Merely as a man, except as the Holy Spirit taught him and used him, the prophet was fallible as other men are fallible. But when the Spirit was upon him, when he was taken up and borne along by the Holy Spirit, he became infallible in his teachings; for his teachings were not his, but the teachings of the Holy Spirit. It was God who was then speaking, not the prophet.

For example, Paul, merely as a man, even as a Christian man, undoubtedly had mistaken notions on many things and was more or less subject to the ideas and opinions of his time. But when he taught as an apostle, under the power of the Holy Spirit, he was infallible; rather, the Spirit who taught through him was infallible, and the teachings that resulted from the Spirit's teaching through him were infallible, as infallible as God. Common sense demands that we carefully distinguish between what Paul may have thought as a man and what he actually taught as an apostle. In the Bible, we have the record of what he taught as an apostle.

Someone may cite as possible exceptions to this statement 1 Corinthians 7:6, 25, where Paul said,

17

> *But I say this as a concession, not as a commandment....Now concerning virgins: I have no commandment from the Lord; yet I give judgment as one whom the Lord in His mercy has made trustworthy.*

There are those who think that Paul does not seem to have been sure here that he had the word of the Lord in this particular matter, but that is not the meaning of the passage. The meaning of verse 6 is that his teaching that he had just given was by way of concession to their weakness, not a commandment as to what they must do. And the teaching of verse 25 is that the Lord, during His earthly life, had given no commandment on this subject, but that Paul was giving his judgment. But he said distinctly that he was giving it as *"one whom the Lord in His mercy has made trustworthy."* Furthermore, in the fortieth verse of the chapter, he distinctly said that he had the Spirit of God in his judgment.

But even if we said that the other interpretation of this passage is the correct one—that Paul was not absolutely sure in this case that he had the word of the Lord and the mind of the Lord—that would only show that where Paul was not absolutely sure that he was teaching in the Holy Spirit he was careful to note the fact. This interpretation would only give additional certainty to all other passages that he wrote.

It is sometimes said that Paul taught in his earlier epistles that the Lord would return during his lifetime, and that in this matter he certainly was mistaken. But Paul never taught this in his earlier epistles or any other epistles—he never taught this anywhere. This assertion is contrary to fact. He did say in 1 Thessalonians, which was his first epistle,

> *Then we who are alive and remain shall be caught up together with them* [that is, the believers who had already died] *in the clouds to meet the Lord in the air. And thus we shall always be with the Lord.*   (*1 Thess. 4:17*)

In this verse, Paul did put himself in the same class with those who were still alive when he wrote the words. He naturally and necessarily did not include himself with those who had already died. But in speaking of the Lord's return, he did not say or even hint that he would still be alive when the Lord returned. It is quite probable that Paul did believe at this time that he might be alive when the Lord returned, *but he never taught that he would be alive.* The attitude of expectancy is the true attitude in all ages for every believer. This was the attitude that Paul took until it was distinctly revealed to him that he would depart before the Lord came. I think it is very probable that Paul was inclined to believe in the earlier part of his ministry that he would live until the coming of the Lord, but the Holy Spirit kept him from teaching this and also kept him from all other errors in his teachings.

THE VERY WORDS WERE GIVEN BY THE HOLY SPIRIT

The fifth thing that the Bible makes clear about the inspiration of the Bible writers is that the Holy

Spirit in them not only gave the thought, but also gave the words in which the thought was to be expressed. We find this very clearly stated in 1 Corinthians 2:13:

> *These things we also speak, not in words which man's wisdom teaches but which the Holy Spirit teaches, comparing spiritual things with spiritual.*

One of the most popular of the false theories of inspiration in our day is that the Holy Spirit was the author of the thought but the Bible writers were left to their own choice of words in the expression of the thought. Therefore, according to this theory, we cannot emphasize the exact meaning of the Bible's words, but we must try to find the thought of God that was behind the words, which the writer more or less inaccurately expressed.

Many teachers in our pulpits and theological seminaries today speak very sneeringly and arrogantly of those who believe in verbal inspiration— that is, the doctrine that the Holy Spirit chose the very words in which the thought He was teaching was to be expressed. But regardless of how contemptuously they may speak of those who believe in verbal inspiration, certainly the Bible claims for itself that it was verbally inspired. The passage that I previously quoted makes it as plain as language can possibly make it that the *"words"* in which the apostle Paul spoke were not *"words which man's wisdom teaches but which the Holy Spirit teaches"* (1 Cor. 2:13).

Now, if this were not the fact, if only the *thought* that was given to Paul was from God and Paul clothed the thought in his own words, then Paul was thoroughly deceived on a fundamental point. In this case, we cannot depend on any point of his teachings. Or, Paul was a deliberate fraud, in which case the quicker we burn up his books, the better for us and all concerned.

Attempts to find a compromise between the two positions have landed those who have tried it in all kinds of absurdities. There is no possibility of finding any middle ground. If you have an exact and logical mind, you must make your choice between verbal inspiration and blatant unbelief. I, for one, must choose verbal inspiration, for Paul distinctly stated that the words in which he conveyed to others the truth that was revealed to him were the words that the Holy Spirit taught him.

The Holy Spirit Himself has anticipated all these ingenious but wholly unbiblical, utterly illogical, and entirely false theories regarding His own work in the Bible writers. The theory that "the concept" was inspired but the words in which the concept was expressed were not was anticipated by the Holy Spirit. He discredited it many centuries before our supposedly wise theological teachers conceived it and attempted to foist it upon an unsuspecting public.

Furthermore, the theory is absurd in itself. The only way thought can be conveyed from one mind to another—from one man's mind to another man's mind, or from the mind of God to the mind of man—is by words; therefore, if the words are imperfect, the thought expressed by those words is also imperfect.

The theory is an absurdity on its very surface, and it is difficult to see how intelligent men could ever have deceived themselves into believing such a thoroughly illogical theory. If the words are not inspired, the Bible is not inspired. Let us not deceive ourselves; let us face facts.

In addition, the more carefully and minutely one studies the *wording* of the statements of this wonderful Book—the Bible—the more he will become convinced of the marvelous accuracy of *the very words* used to express the thought. To a superficial thinker, the doctrine of verbal inspiration may appear questionable or even absurd. But any regenerate and Spirit-taught individual who ponders the words of Scripture day by day, and year after year, will become thoroughly and immovably convinced that the wisdom of God is in *the very words* used as well as in the thought that is expressed in the words.

It is a significant and deeply impressive fact that our difficulties with the Bible rapidly disappear as we note the precise language used. The changing of a word or letter, or a tense, case, or number, would often land us in contradiction or untruth. But as we take the words *exactly as written in the original manuscripts,* difficulties disappear and truth shines forth. Countless times people have come to me with apparent difficulties and supposed contradictions in the Bible and have asked for a solution. I have pointed them to the exact words used, and the solution was found in taking the words exactly as written. It was because they changed in a slight degree the very words that God spoke that a difficulty had seemed to arise.

The divine origin of nature shines forth more clearly the closer we examine it under a microscope. By the use of a powerful microscope, we see the perfection of form in the minutest particles of matter. We are overwhelmingly convinced that God, a God of infinite wisdom and power, a wisdom extending down to the minutest parts of matter, is the author of the material universe. Likewise, the divine origin of the Bible shines forth more and more clearly under close inspection. The more intently we study the Bible, the more we note the perfection with which the turn of a word reveals the absolute thought of God.

An important question—and a question that has puzzled many writers at this point—is this: If the Holy Spirit is the author of the very words of Scripture, how do we account for the variations in style and wording? How is it, for example, that Paul always used Pauline language, that John always used Johannine language, and so on? The answer to this question is very simple and is twofold.

First, even if we could not account at all for this fact, it would have little weight against the explicit statements of God's Word. Anyone who is humble and wise will recognize that there are a great many things that he cannot account for at all that could be easily accounted for if he knew a little more. It is only the man who has such amazing and astounding conceit that he thinks he knows as much as God—in other words, that he is infinite in wisdom—who will reject an explicit statement of God's Word simply because he sees a difficulty within it that he in his limited knowledge cannot solve.

But there is a second answer, and an all-sufficient one, and it is this: these variations in style and wording are easily accounted for because the Holy Spirit is infinitely wise. He Himself is the creator of man and of man's power of speech; therefore, He is wise enough and has quite enough skill in the use of language that, when revealing truth to and through any individual, He uses words, phrases, and forms of expression that are in that person's ordinary vocabulary and forms of thought. He is also quite wise enough to make use of that person's individuality in revealing the truth through him. It is one of the marks of the divine wisdom of this Book that the same divine truth is expressed with absolute accuracy in such widely different forms of expression.

EVERY SCRIPTURE IS INSPIRED BY GOD

The sixth thing that the Bible makes plain regarding the work of the Holy Spirit in the various writers of Scripture, is that all Scripture—that is, everything contained in all the books of the Old and New Testaments—is inspired by God. We are distinctly taught this truth in 2 Timothy 3:16–17. Here we read,

> *All Scripture* [more exactly, "every Scripture"] *is given by inspiration of God* [more literally, "is God-breathed"], *and is profitable for doctrine* [or teaching], *for reproof, for correction, for instruction in righteousness* [rather, instruction that is in righteousness], *that the man of God may be complete, thoroughly*

> *equipped* [better, "equipped completely"] *for every good work.*

In the Revised Version, an attempt has been made to obscure the full force of these words. In this translation, the words are rendered as follows:

> *Every Scripture inspired of God is also profitable for teaching, for reproof, for correction, for instruction which is in righteousness: that the man of God may be complete, furnished completely unto every good work.*

There is absolutely no warrant in the Greek text for changing "[Every] *Scripture is given by inspiration of God, and is profitable for* [teaching]" to *"Every Scripture inspired of God is also profitable for teaching."* "Every" is in the Greek. There is no "is" in the Greek. It must be supplied, as is often the case in translating from Greek into English. "Is" must be supplied somewhere, either before *"given by inspiration"* or after it. But if the "is" is placed after it, "and" must be changed to "also" (a change that is possible but very uncommon). Furthermore, there is not a single instance in the New Testament outside of this one in which two adjectives coupled by "and" are ripped apart and the "is" is placed between them and the "and" is changed to "also." On the other hand, the other construction, "[Every] *Scripture is given by inspiration of God, and is profitable for* [teaching]," is not at all uncommon. So we see that the translation of the Revised Version does violence to all customary usage of the Greek language.

But we do not need to dwell on that, for, even if we accept the changes given in the Revised Version, the thought is not essentially changed. If Paul had said what the Revised Version makes him say, that *"Every Scripture inspired of God is also profitable for teaching,"* there can be no question that by *"every Scripture inspired of God"* he referred to every Scripture contained in the Old Testament. Here, then, taking whichever translation you will, we have the plain teaching that every Scripture of the Old Testament is "God-breathed" or *"inspired of God."* Certainly, if we can believe this about the Old Testament, there is no difficulty in believing it about the New.

Furthermore, there can be no question that Paul claimed for his own teaching an authority equal to that of Old Testament teaching. This we will see clearly in the next section of this chapter. And not only did Paul claim this, but the apostle Peter also classified the teaching of Paul with Old Testament teaching as being Scripture. Peter said in 2 Peter 3:15–16,

> As also our beloved brother Paul, according to the wisdom given to him, has written to you, as also in all his epistles, speaking in them of these things, in which are some things hard to understand, which untaught and unstable people twist to their own destruction, as they do also the rest of the Scriptures.

Here Peter clearly spoke of Paul's epistles as being Scripture.

THE BIBLE IS GOD'S INERRANT WORD

The seventh thing that the Bible teaches concerning the extent of the inspiration of its writings is that, because of this inspiration of the writers of the Bible, the whole Bible as originally given is the absolutely inerrant Word of God. In the Old Testament, David said of his own writings, in a passage already referred to, *"The Spirit of the LORD spoke by me, and His word was on my tongue"* (2 Sam. 23:2). In Mark 7:13, our Lord Jesus Himself called the Law of Moses *"the word of God."* He said, *"making the word of God of no effect through your tradition which you have handed down."* In the verses immediately preceding, He had been drawing a contrast between the teachings of the Mosaic Law (not merely the teachings of the Ten Commandments, but other parts of the Mosaic Law as well) and the traditions of the scribes and Pharisees. He had shown how the traditions of the scribes and Pharisees flatly contradicted the requirements of the Law as given through Moses. In summing up the matter, He said in the verse just quoted that the scribes and Pharisees invalidated *"the word of God"* by their traditions, thus calling the Law of Moses *"the word of God."*

When I was in England, a high dignitary and scholar in the Church of England wrote me a private letter in which he tried to reprimand me by saying that the Bible nowhere claims to be the Word of God. I replied to him by showing him that not only does the Bible claim it, but the Lord Jesus Himself said in so many words that the Law given through Moses was *"the word of God."*

In 1 Thessalonians 2:13, the apostle Paul claimed that his own epistles and teachings are *"the word of God."* He said,

> *For this reason we also thank God without ceasing, because when you received the word of God which you heard from us, you welcomed it not as the word of men, but as it is in truth, the word of God, which also effectively works in you who believe.*

Here the apostle Paul claimed in the most absolute way that his own teachings are *"the word of God."*

When we read the words of Jeremiah, Isaiah, Paul, John, James, Jude, and the other Bible writers, we are reading what God says. We are not listening to the voice of man, but we are listening to the voice of God. The Word of God, which we have in the Old and New Testaments, is absolutely inerrant as originally given—down to the smallest word and smallest letter or part of a letter. In Matthew 5:18, our Lord Jesus Himself said of the Pentateuch (the first five books of the Bible), *"For assuredly, I say to you, till heaven and earth pass away, one jot or one tittle will by no means pass from the law till all is fulfilled."* Now, a *"jot"* is the Hebrew character *yodh*, the smallest character in the Hebrew alphabet, less than half the size of any other letter in the Hebrew alphabet. A *"tittle"* is a part of a letter, the little horn put on some of the Hebrew consonants, less than the cross we put on a "t." Here our Lord said that the

Law given through Moses is absolutely inerrant, down to its smallest letter or part of a letter. That certainly is verbal inspiration with a vengeance.

Again, Jesus said, as recorded in John 10:35, after having quoted from Psalm 82:6 as conclusive proof of a point, *"The Scripture **cannot be broken"*** (emphasis added). Thus He asserted the absolute inerrancy and finality of the Scriptures. If the Scriptures as originally given are not the inerrant Word of God, then not only is the Bible a fraud, but Jesus Christ Himself was utterly misled and is therefore utterly unreliable as a teacher.

I have said that the Scriptures of the Old and New Testaments *as originally given* were absolutely inerrant. Of course, the following question arises: To what extent are the modern translations the inerrant Word of God? The answer is simple: they are the inerrant Word of God just to the extent that they are an accurate rendering of the Scriptures of the Old and New Testaments as originally given. There are, it is true, many variations in the many manuscripts we possess—thousands of variations. But by a careful study of these variations, we are able to find with marvelous accuracy what the original manuscripts said. A very large share of the variations are of no importance whatsoever, since it is evident from a comparison of different manuscripts that they are the mistakes of a transcriber. Many other variations simply concern the order of the words used, and in translating into English, in which the order of words is often different from what it is in the Greek, the variation is not translatable. Many other variations are of small Greek particles, many of which are not translatable into English anyway. When all the variations of any significance have been reduced to the minimum to which it is possible to reduce them by a careful study of manuscripts, not one single variation is left that affects any doctrine held by the evangelical churches.

Who Is the
God of the Bible?

2

Who Is the God of the Bible?

God is Spirit.
—John 4:24

God is light.
—1 John 1:5

God is love.
—1 John 4:8, 16

The texts above give three of the most remarkable statements that were ever uttered. In the clearest possible way, they set before us the Christian understanding of God as distinguished from every other understanding of God.

Many wrong ideas about God are being promoted today. The Christian Scientists are one group that is spreading falsehood. They constantly quote one of our texts: *"God is love"*; in fact, they quote it more than almost any other passage in the Bible. But by *"God is love"* they do not mean at all what 1 John 4:8 or 1 John 4:16 clearly mean when taken in their context. By *"love"* the Christian Scientists do not mean a personal attribute of God; they mean an impersonal, abstract quality that is itself

God. Mary Baker Eddy, the founder of Christian Science, frankly and flatly denied that God is a person.

Not only do the Christian Scientists say, *"God is love,"* but they also say, "Love is God." Not only do they say, *"God is good"* (Ps. 73:1), but they also say, "Good is God." Saying "Love is God" is entirely different from saying *"God is love."* You might as well say, "Spirit is God," because the Bible says, *"God is Spirit."* However, we know that all spirit is not God. Or you might as well say, "Light is God," because the Bible says, *"God is light."* However, we know that light is not God. In the same way, love is not God, though *"God is love."*

What is meant by *"love"* in the inspired statement *"God is love"*? The answer is shown by the definition or description of love given in the context and in a passage in the immediately preceding chapter—1 John 3:13–18. These verses clearly show that the statement in 1 John 4:8 and 1 John 4:16, *"God is love,"* does not mean that God is an abstract quality called love and that the abstract quality of love is God. It means that God is a person whose whole being and conduct are dominated by the quality of love, that is, by a desire for and delight in the highest welfare of others. This fact will be evident to you if you read the passage from 1 John 3:

> *Do not marvel, my brethren, if the world hates you. We know that we have passed from death to life, because we love the brethren. He who does not love his brother abides in death. Whoever hates his brother is a murderer, and you know that no murderer has eternal life abiding*

*in him. By this we know love, because He laid
down His life for us. And we also ought to lay
down our lives for the brethren. But whoever
has this world's goods, and sees his brother in
need, and shuts up his heart from him, how
does the love of God abide in him? My little
children, let us not love in word or in tongue,
but in deed and in truth.   (1 John 3:13–18)*

This fact is also evident from the context of the
chapter of our text—1 John 4:

*Beloved, let us love one another, for love is of
God; and everyone who loves is born of God
and knows God. He who does not love does not
know God, for God is love. In this the love of
God was manifested toward us, that God has
sent His only begotten Son into the world, that
we might live through Him. In this is love, not
that we loved God, but that He loved us and
sent His Son to be the propitiation for our sins.
Beloved, if God so loved us, we also ought to
love one another. No one has seen God at any
time. If we love one another, God abides in us,
and His love has been perfected in us. By this
we know that we abide in Him, and He in us,
because He has given us of His Spirit. And we
have seen and testify that the Father has sent
the Son as Savior of the world. Whoever confesses that Jesus is the Son of God, God abides
in him, and he in God. And we have known
and believed the love that God has for us. God
is love, and he who abides in love abides in
God, and God in him. Love has been perfected*

*among us in this: that we may have boldness
in the day of judgment; because as He is, so
are we in this world.*   *(1 John 4:7–17)*

Along with Christian Science, modern philosophy also spreads false ideas about God. The God of modern philosophy is sometimes called "The Absolute." What is generally meant by "The Absolute" is a cold, abstract thing, not a dear, definite, warm Person who loves others and grieves, suffers, and works intelligently for them. Modern philosophy often teaches that not only is God *in* all things but God *is* all things and all things are God. Such a God is no God at all. However, the God of the Bible, as we will see as we proceed, is a divine Person who exists apart from the world that He created and who existed before the world that He created. The God of the Bible is actively involved in the world He has made, and He works along definite and clearly revealed lines.

In addition, many political leaders are fond of talking about God, but if anyone will carefully study their words, it often becomes plain that by "God" they do not mean the God and Father of our Lord Jesus Christ.

So we come face to face with the question, What sort of a being is the God of the Bible, the one true God, the only God whom we should worship, love, and obey?

GOD IS SPIRIT

First of all, *"God is Spirit"* (John 4:24). This we read in our first text. Notice that the King James

Version says, *"God is a Spirit."* However, there is no indefinite article in the Greek language. Wherever an indefinite article is necessary in an English translation to fit the English idiom, it has to be supplied, and it is supplied in this case. But there is no more reason for supplying it here than for supplying it in 1 John 4:8 and saying "God is a love," or in 1 John 1:5 and saying "God is a light." The preferable translation is as I have given it: *"God is Spirit."*

What Is Meant by *"Spirit"*?

"God is Spirit" is a definition of the essential nature of God. What does it mean? Our Lord Jesus Himself defined what is meant by *"spirit"* in Luke 24:39, where He is recorded as saying after His resurrection, *"Behold My hands and My feet, that it is I Myself. Handle Me and see, for a spirit does not have flesh and bones as you see I have."* It is evident from these words of our Lord that *"spirit"* is that which is contrasted with body. That is to say, *"spirit"* is invisible reality. To say that *"God is Spirit"* (John 4:24) is to say that God is essentially incorporeal (without a material body) and invisible (see 1 Timothy 6:16), that God in His essential nature is not material but immaterial and invisible, but nevertheless real.

This thought is also found in the very heart of the revelation that God made of Himself to Moses in the Old Testament. We read in the book of Deuteronomy,

> *Take careful heed to yourselves, for you saw no form when the LORD spoke to you at Horeb out*

*of the midst of the fire, lest you act corruptly
and make for yourselves a carved image in the
form of any figure: the likeness of male or fe-
male, the likeness of any animal that is on the
earth or the likeness of any winged bird that
flies in the air, the likeness of anything that
creeps on the ground or the likeness of any fish
that is in the water beneath the earth.*

(Deut. 4:15–18)

Fifteen centuries before Christ, this is a plain declaration of the spirituality of God in His essential nature. God is essentially invisible spirit.

Can God Be Seen with the Human Eye?

Spirit, however, may be manifested in visible,
bodily form. This fact is clearly revealed in the Word
of God. We read in John 1:32 these words of John
the Baptist about what his own eyes had seen: *"And
John bare witness, saying, I have beheld the Spirit
descending as a dove out of heaven; and it abode
upon him* [Jesus]" (RV). Here, then, we see God the
Holy Spirit, who is essentially spirit, manifesting
Himself in a bodily, visible form.

Furthermore, we are told in the Bible that God
the Father has manifested Himself in visible form.
We read in Exodus,

*Then Moses went up, also Aaron, Nadab, and
Abihu, and seventy of the elders of Israel, and
they saw the God of Israel. And there was under
His feet as it were a paved work of sapphire*

38

> *stone, and it was like the very heavens in its*
> *clarity.* (Exod. 24:9–10)

What they saw was not God in His essential nature as spiritual being. Indeed, what we see when we see one another is not our essential selves, but the houses we live in. Therefore, John could say, as he did in John 1:18: *"No one has seen God at any time."* Similarly, I could say that no one has ever seen me. Nevertheless, it was a real manifestation of God Himself that they saw. It could be said, and said truthfully, that they had seen God, even as it could be said truthfully that people have seen me.

Furthermore, though God is essentially spirit, He has a visible form. This is taught in the most unmistakable terms in Philippians 2:6, where we are told that our Lord Jesus existed originally *"in the form of God."* The Greek word that is translated *"form"* in this passage means "visible form," "the form by which a person or thing strikes the vision," "the external appearance." It cannot mean anything else. This is the definition given in the best Greek-English lexicon of the New Testament. Now, since Jesus existed originally *"in the form of God,"* it is evident that God Himself must have a form, this form in which our Lord Jesus is said to have existed originally.

That God in His external form, though not in His invisible essence, is *seeable,* is also clear from Acts 7:55–56, where we read,

> *But he* [Stephen], *being full of the Holy Spirit,*
> *gazed into heaven and saw the glory of God,*
> *and Jesus standing at the right hand of God,*

*and said, "Look! I see the heavens opened and
the Son of Man standing at the right hand of
God!"*

Now, if God does not have a form that can be seen,
then, of course, the Lord Jesus could not be seen
standing at His right hand. As we will see later, God
is everywhere, but God is not everywhere *in the
same sense.* There is a place where God is visibly and
clearly present in a way in which He is not present
anywhere else.

Does God Live in Heaven?

Although in His spiritual presence God pervades
the universe, the place of God's visible presence and
full manifestation of Himself is heaven. This fact is
evident from many passages in the Scriptures. For
example, it is clear from the prayer that our Lord
taught us—a portion of Scripture accepted by many
who reject most of the Bible. Our Lord began the
prayer that He taught His disciples with these
words: *"Our Father which art in heaven"* (Matt. 6:9
KJV). If these words mean anything, they certainly
mean that God our Father is in heaven in a way in
which He is not elsewhere. That was where God was
when Jesus was addressing Him. We read in Matthew 3:17, *"Suddenly a voice came from heaven, saying, 'This is My beloved Son, in whom I am well
pleased.'"* If these words mean anything, they mean
that God is in heaven and that His voice came out of
the heavens to the Lord Jesus who was here on
earth.

Again, in John 14:28, Jesus is recorded as saying,

You have heard Me say to you, "I am going away and coming back to you." If you loved Me, you would rejoice because I said, "I am going to the Father," for My Father is greater than I.

Taken in the light of the events that were to follow, these words, if they mean anything, mean that Jesus was going away from the place where He was then—earth—to another place—heaven. Furthermore, in going to heaven, He was going to where God is, and He was leaving earth, where God is not present in the sense in which He is in heaven.

We read in Acts 11:9: *"But the voice answered me again from heaven, 'What God has cleansed you must not call common.'"* Here, again, God is represented as speaking from heaven, where He was.

Again, our Lord Jesus Christ is recorded in John 20:17 as saying to Mary Magdalene after His resurrection,

Do not cling to Me, for I have not yet ascended to My Father; but go to My brethren and say to them, "I am ascending to My Father and your Father, and to My God and your God."

From this it is unmistakably evident that there is a place where God is, a place to which Jesus was going after His resurrection. That place is in heaven. There is no possibility of explaining this away by

41

saying that Jesus was using a figure of speech. The whole passage loses its meaning by any such interpretation, and to attempt to so explain it is a trick and a deception that will not bear close examination.

Moreover, the apostle Paul told us regarding our Lord Jesus Christ that God the Father *"raised Him from the dead and seated Him at His right hand in the heavenly places"* (Eph. 1:20). This verse makes it as clear as language can make anything that there is a place called heaven where God is in a sense that He is nowhere else, and where one can be placed at His right hand.

The same thing is evident from the verses that I already quoted when talking about God in His external form—Acts 7:55–56. Here we are told that Stephen,

> *being full of the Holy Spirit, gazed into heaven and saw the glory of God, and Jesus standing at the right hand of God, and said, "Look! I see the heavens opened and the Son of Man standing at the right hand of God!"*

The meaning of these words—to anybody who wishes to know what words are intended to convey and does not merely wish to distort them to fit his own theories—is that God is, in a special sense, present in heaven. There is no escaping this truth by any fair, honest interpretation.

Men who are skillful in the art of discrediting truth by assigning it improper names—names that sound very scholarly—may call this precious truth found in Acts 7:55–56 *anthropomorphism* (which means "attributing qualities of personhood to something that is not a person"). That sounds very learned. Nevertheless, whether it is anthropomorphism or what not, this truth is the clear teaching of the Word of God, in spite of frightful terms used to scare immature college students. There is no mistaking that this truth that God is in heaven is the teaching of the Bible, and we have already proven that the Bible is God's Word. As such, it is to be taken at its face value, in spite of all the attempts to explain it away—attempts made by men and women who profess to be wise but have become fools (Rom. 1:22).

GOD IS A PERSON

The next thing that the Bible teaches about God is that God is a person. That is to say, He is a being who knows, feels, loves, speaks, acts, and hears. He is a being who interacts intelligently with us and with whom we can interact.

While God is in all things, He is a person distinct from the persons and things in which He is. He has created these persons and things. The Bible, both in the Old and New Testaments, is full of this vital teaching of "a living God" as distinguished from the mere cold ideas of "The Absolute" or "The Infinite" or "The Supreme Being" or "The Great First Cause," all of which modern philosophy loves to promote.

For example, we read in Jeremiah,

> But the LORD is the true God; He is the living
> God and the everlasting King. At His wrath

the earth will tremble, and the nations will not be able to endure His indignation. Thus you shall say to them: "The gods that have not made the heavens and the earth shall perish from the earth and from under these heavens." He has made the earth by His power, He has established the world by His wisdom, and has stretched out the heavens at His discretion. When He utters His voice, there is a multitude of waters in the heavens: "and He causes the vapors to ascend from the ends of the earth. He makes lightning for the rain, He brings the wind out of His treasuries." Everyone is dull-hearted, without knowledge; every metalsmith is put to shame by an image; for his molded image is falsehood, and there is no breath in them. They are futile, a work of errors; in the time of their punishment they shall perish. The Portion of Jacob is not like them, for He is the Maker of all things, and Israel is the tribe of His inheritance; the LORD *of hosts is His name.* (Jer. 10:10–16)

In this passage, God is distinguished from idols, which are things and not persons—things that *"cannot speak," "cannot go," "cannot do evil, nor can they do any good"* (Jer. 10:5). We are also told that Jehovah is wiser than *"all the wise men"* (v. 7). Is *"the living God," "the everlasting King,"* who has *"wrath"* and *"indignation"* (v. 10), separate from His creatures? The answer is found in the same verse: *"At His wrath the earth will tremble, and the nations will not be able to endure His indignation"* (v. 10).

In the New Testament, we find another example of the wonderful truth that God is a person. In the fourteenth chapter of Acts, the people of Lystra observed a miracle performed by Paul and supposed that he and Barnabas were gods. As the people were about to sacrifice to Paul and Barnabas, the two men cried out,

> *Men, why are you doing these things? We also are men with the same nature as you, and preach to you that you should turn from these useless things* [false gods, idols] *to the living God, who made the heaven, the earth, the sea, and all things that are in them.* *(Acts 14:15)*

Here, also, we have the representation of God as a personal being distinct from His created work, and also clearly distinct from idols, which are not living gods. In addition, in 1 Thessalonians 1:9, the converts at Thessalonica are represented as turning from *"idols* [dead gods] *to serve the living and true God"* (emphasis added).

In 2 Chronicles 16:9, we are told that *"the eyes of the LORD run to and fro throughout the whole earth, to show Himself strong on behalf of those whose heart is loyal to Him."* In Psalm 94:9–10, we read, *"He who planted the ear, shall He not hear? He who formed the eye, shall He not see? He who instructs the nations, shall He not correct?"* These are clearly descriptions of a personal God, not a mere abstract idea, such as "The Absolute" or "The Infinite" or "The Supreme Being."

The distinction between God, who is present in all things and dwells in all believers, and the things and persons in which He dwells, is brought out very clearly by our Lord Himself in John 14:10. Here Jesus revealed that He is one with the Father, but that the Father works within Him independently as a separate person:

> *Do you not believe that I am in the Father, and the Father in Me? The words that I speak to you I do not speak on My own authority; but the Father who dwells in Me does the works.*

In the twenty-fourth verse of the same chapter, our Lord Jesus again distinguished between His own personhood and that of the Father, who dwelt in Him, in these words: *"He who does not love Me does not keep My words; and the word which you hear is not Mine but the Father's who sent Me."*

This understanding of God pervades the entire Bible. The view of God presented in the Bible is entirely different from the view of God presented in pantheism, Buddhism, Theosophy,* and Christian Science. The correct understanding of God is found in the opening words of the Bible: *"In the beginning God created the heavens and the earth"* (Gen. 1:1). Here the God of the Bible is clearly differentiated from the so-called God of pantheism and the so-called God of Christian Science. The proper understanding of God is also found in the last chapter of the Bible, and it is found in every chapter of the Bible between the first and the last. The God of the

---

* Theosophy is the teaching of a movement that originated in the U.S. in 1875 and that follows primarily Buddhistic and Hindu theories, especially of pantheistic evolution and reincarnation.

Bible is a personal being who, while He created all things and is in all things, is a distinct person, separate from the persons and things He has created.

GOD IS ACTIVELY INVOLVED IN THE WORLD

We turn now to a consideration of the present relationship of this personal God to the world that He has created and to the people whom He has created.

In the first place, we find that God sustains, governs, and cares for the world He has created. He shapes the whole present history of the world. This comes out in the Bible again and again. A few illustrations must suffice. We read in the book of Psalms,

> *These all wait for You, that You may give them their food in due season. What You give them they gather in; You open Your hand, they are filled with good. You hide Your face, they are troubled; You take away their breath, they die and return to their dust. You send forth Your Spirit, they are created; and You renew the face of the earth.* (Ps. 104:27–30)

We read in Psalm 75:6–7, *"For exaltation comes neither from the east nor from the west nor from the south. But God is the Judge: He puts down one, and exalts another."* These passages, along with others that could be cited, set forth God's present relationship to the world that He has created.

Now let us look at God's relationship to the concerns of people. We will find that God has a present, personal interest and an active hand in the concerns

of people. He makes a path for His own people and
leads them. He delivers, saves, and punishes.

To prove this point, four illustrations from the
Bible will suffice. First of all, we read in Joshua,

> *And Joshua said, "By this you shall know that
> the living God is among you, and that He will
> without fail drive out from before you the Ca-
> naanites and the Hittites and the Hivites and
> the Perizzites and the Girgashites and the
> Amorites and the Jebusites."*   *(Josh. 3:10)*

Now we will look at a passage in Daniel:

> *And when he* [the king] *came to the den, he
> cried out with a lamenting voice to Daniel.
> The king spoke, saying to Daniel, "Daniel,
> servant of the living God, has your God, whom
> you serve continually, been able to deliver you
> from the lions?" Then Daniel said to the king,
> "O king, live forever! My God sent His angel
> and shut the lions' mouths, so that they have
> not hurt me, because I was found innocent be-
> fore Him; and also, O king, I have done no
> wrong before you."...Then King Darius
> wrote:...I make a decree that in every domin-
> ion of my kingdom men must tremble and fear
> before the God of Daniel. For He is the living
> God, and steadfast forever; His kingdom is the
> one which shall not be destroyed, and His do-
> minion shall endure to the end. He delivers
> and rescues, and He works signs and wonders
> in heaven and on earth, who has delivered
> Daniel from the power of the lions.*
>   *(Dan. 6:20–22, 25–27)*

First Timothy 4:10 provides the third illustration: *"For to this end we both labor and suffer reproach, because we trust in the living God, who is the Savior of all men, especially of those who believe."*

Now we will look at some verses in Hebrews:

> *Anyone who has rejected Moses' law dies without mercy on the testimony of two or three witnesses. Of how much worse punishment, do you suppose, will he be thought worthy who has trampled the Son of God underfoot, counted the blood of the covenant by which he was sanctified a common thing, and insulted the Spirit of grace? For we know Him who said, "Vengeance is Mine, I will repay," says the Lord. And again, "The LORD will judge His people." It is a fearful thing to fall into the hands of the living God.* (Heb. 10:28–31)

In all these passages, we have this same concept of God in His relationship to man, namely, that God has a personal interest and an active hand in the concerns of people. He makes a path for His own people and leads them. He delivers, saves, and punishes.

The God of the Bible is to be clearly distinguished, not merely from the God of the pantheists, who has no existence separate from His creation, but also from the God of the deists, who has created the world, put into it all the necessary powers of self-government and development, set it going, and left it to go by itself. The God of the Bible is a God who is personally and actively present in the affairs of the universe today. He sustains, governs, and cares for the world He has created; He shapes the whole present history of the world. He has a present, personal interest and an active hand in the concerns of people, and it is He who is behind all the events that are occurring today. He reigns and makes even the wrath of men to praise Him, and the remainder of wrath He restrains (Ps. 76:10 KJV).

Armies may clash, force and violence and outrage may seem victorious for the passing hour, but God stands triumphant over all. Through all the confusion and the discord and the turmoil and the agony and the ruin, through all the outrageous atrocities that are making men's hearts stand still with horror, He is carrying out His own purposes of love and making all things work together for good to those who love Him (Rom. 8:28).

Is God Perfect, and Is He One?

3

Is God Perfect, and Is He One?

God is light and in Him is no darkness at all.
—1 John 1:5

God is love.
—1 John 4:8, 16

With God all things are possible.
—Matthew 19:26

His understanding is infinite.
—Psalm 147:5

I n this chapter, we will continue to consider the Christian understanding of God. We saw in the previous chapter that God is spirit, that God is a person, and that God has a personal interest and an active hand in the concerns of people today. He sustains, governs, and cares for the world He has created, and He shapes the whole present history of the world.

THE INFINITE PERFECTION OF GOD

The next thing to be observed about the Christian understanding of God is that God is perfect and infinite in power and in all His intellectual and moral attributes.

God Is Light

First of all, fix your attention on the first part of our first text: *"God is light"* (1 John 1:5). These three words form a marvelously beautiful and overwhelmingly impressive statement of the truth. They set forth the absolute holiness and perfect wisdom of God. These three words need to be meditated on rather than expounded. *"In Him is no darkness at all"* (v. 5). That is to say, in God is no darkness of error, no darkness of ignorance, no darkness of sin, no darkness of moral imperfection or intellectual imperfection of any kind. The three words *"God is light"* form one of the most beautiful, one of the most striking, and one of the most stupendous statements of truth that has ever been penned.

God Is Omnipotent

Second, the God of the Bible is omnipotent, or all-powerful. This wonderful fact comes out again and again in the Word of God. One direct statement of this great truth, which is especially striking because of the context in which it is found, is in Jeremiah 32:17:

Ah, Lord GOD! Behold, You have made the heavens and the earth by Your great power and outstretched arm. There is nothing too hard for You.

Here Jeremiah said that there is nothing too diffi-cult for God, but in the twenty-seventh verse, Jeho-vah Himself said, *"Behold, I am the LORD, the God of all flesh. Is there anything too hard for Me?"*

When at last Job had been brought to see and to recognize the true nature of Jehovah, he said, *"I know that You can do everything, and that no pur-pose of Yours can be withheld from You"* (Job 42:2). In Matthew 19:26, our Lord Jesus said, *"With God all things are possible."*

So we are plainly taught by our Lord Himself and by others that God can do all things, that noth-ing is too hard for Him, that all things are possible with Him—in a word, that God is omnipotent.

Here is a very impressive passage from the book of Psalms that sets forth this same great truth:

> *By the word of the LORD the heavens were made, and all the host of them by the breath of His mouth. He gathers the waters of the sea together as a heap; He lays up the deep in storehouses. Let all the earth fear the LORD; let all the inhabitants of the world stand in awe of Him. For He spoke, and it was done; He com-manded, and it stood fast.* (Ps. 33:6–9)

Here we see God, by the mere utterance of His voice, bringing to pass anything that He desires to be brought to pass.

We find this same majestic portrayal of God in the very first chapter of the Bible. So many people who imagine themselves to be scholarly are telling us this chapter is out-of-date, yet it contains some of

the sublimest words that were ever written, un-
matched by anything that any philosopher, scientist,
or orator is saying today. The very first words of this
chapter read, *"In the beginning God created the
heavens and the earth"* (Gen. 1:1). This description
of the origin of things has never been matched for
simplicity, sublimity, and profundity. In the third
verse, we read, *"Then God said, 'Let there be light';
and there was light."* These words need no comment.
In this verse, there is a sublime thought about the
omnipotence of God's mere word, before which any
truly intelligent and alert soul will stand in wonder
and awe. Nothing in poetry or in philosophical dis-
sertation, ancient or modern, can for one moment
compare with these sublime words.

Over and over again, the thought is brought out
in the Word of God that all nature is absolutely subject to God's will and word. We see this, for example,
in the book of Psalms:

> *For He commands and raises the stormy wind,
> which lifts up the waves of the sea. They* [the
> sailors] *mount up to the heavens, they go down
> again to the depths; their soul melts because of
> trouble. They reel to and fro, and stagger like
> a drunken man, and are at their wits' end.
> Then they cry out to the LORD in their trouble,
> and He brings them out of their distresses. He
> calms the storm, so that its waves are still.*
> *(Ps. 107:25–29)*

A similar description is found in the book of Na-
hum:

> *The LORD is slow to anger and great in power,
> and will not at all acquit the wicked. The
> LORD has His way in the whirlwind and in
> the storm, and the clouds are the dust of His
> feet. He rebukes the sea and makes it dry, and
> dries up all the rivers. Bashan and Carmel
> wither, and the flower of Lebanon wilts. The
> mountains quake before Him, the hills melt,
> and the earth heaves at His presence, yes, the
> world and all who dwell in it. Who can stand
> before His indignation? And who can endure
> the fierceness of His anger? His fury is poured
> out like fire, and the rocks are thrown down by
> Him.   (Nah. 1:3–6)*

What a picture we have here of the omnipotence and
awe-inspiring majesty of God!

Not only is nature shown to be absolutely subject to God's will and word, but men also are shown
to be absolutely subject to His will and word. For
example, we read in the book of James,

> *There is one Lawgiver, who is able to save and
> to destroy. Who are you to judge another?
> Come now, you who say, "Today or tomorrow
> we will go to such and such a city, spend a
> year there, buy and sell, and make a profit";
> whereas you do not know what will happen
> tomorrow. For what is your life? It is even a
> vapor that appears for a little time and then
> vanishes away. Instead you ought to say, "If
> the Lord wills, we shall live and do this or
> that."   (James 4:12–15)*

Happy is the man who voluntarily subjects himself to God's will and word. But whether we voluntarily subject ourselves or not, we are subject. The angels are also subject to His will and word (Heb. 1:13–14). Even Satan himself, though entirely against his own will, is absolutely subject to the will and word of God, as is evident from Job 1:12 and Job 2:6.

The exercise of God's omnipotence is limited by His own wise and holy and loving will. God *can* do anything but *will* do only what infinite wisdom, holiness, and love dictate. This comes out, for example, in Isaiah 59:1–2:

> *Behold, the Lord's hand is not shortened, that it cannot save; nor His ear heavy, that it cannot hear. But your iniquities have separated you from your God; and your sins have hidden His face from you, so that He will not hear.*

God Is Omniscient

The God of the Bible is also omniscient, or all-knowing. In 1 John 3:20, we read, *"God...knows all things."* Turning to the Old Testament, we read, *"Great is our Lord, and mighty in power; His understanding is infinite"* (Ps. 147:5). The literal translation of the last clause of this passage is "of His understanding there is no number." In these passages, it is plainly declared that God knows everything and that His understanding is inexhaustible.

In Job 37:16, Elihu, the messenger of God, said that Jehovah is *"perfect in knowledge."* Along the same lines, in Acts 15:18, we read, *"Known to God from eternity are all His works."* In Psalm 147:4, we are told that *"He counts the number of the stars; He calls them all by name,"* while in Matthew 10:29, we are told that *"not one* [sparrow] *falls to the ground apart from your Father's will."* The stars in all their magnitude and the sparrows in all their insignificance are equally in His mind.

We are further told that everything has a part in God's purpose and plan. In Acts 3:17–18, the apostle Peter said of the crucifixion of our Lord, the wickedest act in all the history of the human race,

> *Yet now, brethren, I know that you did it in ignorance, as did also your rulers. But those things which God foretold by the mouth of all His prophets, that the Christ would suffer, He has thus fulfilled.*

In addition, Peter had declared on the Day of Pentecost that the Lord Jesus was *"delivered* [up] *by the determined purpose and foreknowledge of God"* (Acts 2:23). According to the words of the psalmist, God takes the acts of the wickedest men into His plans and causes the wrath of men to praise Him, and the remainder of wrath He restrains (Ps. 76:10 KJV).

For example, even war with all its horrors, with all its atrocities, with all its abominations, is foreknown by God and taken into His own gracious plan of the ages. He will make every event, even the most shocking things designed by the vilest conspiracy of Devil-inspired men, work together for the good of those who love God and are called according to His purpose (Rom. 8:28).

The whole plan of the ages—not merely of the centuries, but of the immeasurable ages of God—and every man's part in it, has been known to God from all eternity. This is made very clear in the book of Ephesians, where we read,

> [God] *made known to us the mystery of His will, according to His good pleasure which He purposed in Himself, that in the dispensation of the fullness of the times He might gather together in one all things in Christ, both which are in heaven and which are on earth; in Him. In Him also we have obtained an inheritance, being predestined according to the purpose of Him who works all things according to the counsel of His will, that we who first trusted in Christ should be to the praise of His glory.*
> *(Eph. 1:9–12)*

And later in the book of Ephesians, we are told,

> *(When you read, you may understand my knowledge in the mystery of Christ), which in other ages was not made known to the sons of men, as it has now been revealed by the Spirit to His holy apostles and prophets: that the Gentiles should be fellow heirs, of the same body, and partakers of His promise in Christ through the gospel, of which I became a minister according to the gift of the grace of God given to me by the effective working of His power. To me, who am less than the least of all the saints, this grace was given, that I should preach among the Gentiles the unsearchable*

*riches of Christ, and to make all see what is
the fellowship of the mystery, which from the
beginning of the ages has been hidden in God
who created all things through Jesus Christ.*

(Eph. 3:4–9)

There are no afterthoughts with God. Everything is seen, known, purposed, and planned from the outset. We may well exclaim, *"Oh, the depth of the riches both of the wisdom and knowledge of God! How unsearchable are His judgments and His ways past finding out!"* (Rom. 11:33). God knows from all eternity what He will do for all eternity.

God Is Omnipresent

Furthermore, not only is God perfect in His intellectual and moral attributes and in power, but He is also omnipresent, or all-present. In Chapter 2 of this book, we saw that God has a particular habitation, that there is a place where He exists and manifests Himself in a way in which He does not manifest Himself everywhere. But while we insist on this clearly revealed truth, we must also never lose sight of the fact that God is everywhere. We find this truth set forth by Paul in his sermon to the Epicurean and Stoic philosophers on Mars Hill:

*God, who made the world and everything in it,
since He is Lord of heaven and earth, does not
dwell in temples made with hands. Nor is He
worshiped with men's hands, as though He
needed anything, since He gives to all life,*

breath, and all things. And He has made from one blood every nation of men to dwell on all the face of the earth, and has determined their preappointed times and the boundaries of their dwellings, so that they should seek the Lord, in the hope that they might grope for Him and find Him, though He is not far from each one of us; for in Him we live and move and have our being, as also some of your own poets have said, "For we are also His offspring."

(Acts 17:24–28)

This thought about God also comes out in the Old Testament. In the book of Psalms, we read,

Where can I go from Your Spirit? Or where can I flee from Your presence? If I ascend into heaven, You are there; if I make my bed in hell, behold, You are there. If I take the wings of the morning, and dwell in the uttermost parts of the sea, even there Your hand shall lead me, and Your right hand shall hold me.

(Ps. 139:7–10)

There is no place where one can flee from God's presence, for God is everywhere. This great truth is set forth in a remarkable way in the book of Jeremiah:

"Am I a God near at hand," says the LORD, *"and not a God afar off? Can anyone hide himself in secret places, so I shall not see him?" says the* LORD; *"do I not fill heaven and earth?" says the* LORD. *(Jer. 23:23–24)*

From these passages, we see that God is all-present. He is in all parts of the universe, and He is near to each individual. In Him each individual lives and moves and has his being (Acts 17:28). God is in every rose and lily and blade of grass.

God Is Eternal

There is one thought in the Christian understanding of God that needs to be placed alongside of His omnipresence, and that is His eternity. God is eternal. His existence had no beginning and will have no ending. He always was, always is, and always will be. God is not only everywhere present in space, but also everywhere present in time. This teaching about God appears constantly in the Bible. We are told in Genesis 21:33 that Abraham *"called on the name of the LORD, the Everlasting God."* In Isaiah 40:28, we read this description of Jehovah:

Have you not known? Have you not heard? The everlasting God, the LORD, the Creator of the ends of the earth, neither faints nor is weary. His understanding is unsearchable.

Here, again, He is called *"the everlasting God."*

Habakkuk set forth the same picture of God. He said, *"Are You not from everlasting, O LORD my God, my Holy One?"* (Hab. 1:12). The psalmist also gave us the same description of God:

Before the mountains were brought forth, or ever You had formed the earth and the world, even from everlasting to everlasting, You are God....For a thousand years in Your sight are like yesterday when it is past, and like a watch in the night. (Ps. 90:2, 4)

We have the same description of God later in the book of Psalms:

O my God, do not take me away in the midst of my days; Your years are throughout all generations. Of old You laid the foundation of the earth, and the heavens are the work of Your hands. They will perish, but You will endure; yes, they will all grow old like a garment; like a cloak You will change them, and they will be changed. But You are the same, and Your years will have no end. (Ps. 102:24–27)

The very name of God—His covenant name, *Jehovah*—sets forth His eternity. He is the eternal *"I AM"* (Exod. 3:14), the One who is, was, and ever will be (Rev. 1:8).

God Is Holy

God is also absolutely and infinitely holy. This is a point of central and fundamental importance in the biblical understanding of God. It comes out in our first text: *"God is light and in Him is no darkness at all"* (1 John 1:5). When John wrote these words, he gave them as the summary of *"the message which we have heard from* [God]*"* (v. 5).

In the vision of Jehovah that was given to Isaiah in the year that King Uzziah died, the *"seraphim"*

(Isa. 6:2), or "burning ones," burning in their own intense holiness, are shown standing before Jehovah with covered faces and covered feet and constantly crying, *"Holy, holy, holy is the LORD of hosts"* (v. 3). And in 1 Peter 1:16, God cries to us, *"Be holy, for I am holy."*

This thought of the infinite and awe-inspiring holiness of God pervades the entire Bible. It underlies everything in it. The entire Mosaic system is built on and is about this fundamental and central truth. The instructions given to Moses, as well as the punishment of those who disobeyed, were intended to teach, emphasize, and burn into the minds and hearts of the Israelites the fundamental truth that God is holy, unapproachably holy. These instructions and punishments included the following: the system of washings; the divisions of the tabernacle; the divisions of the people into ordinary Israelites, Levites, priests, and high priests, who were all permitted different degrees of approach to God under strictly defined conditions; insistence on blood sacrifices as the necessary medium of approach to God; the strict orders to Israel in regard to approaching Mount Sinai when Jehovah came down upon it; God's directions to Moses in Exodus 3:5 and to Joshua in Joshua 5:15 to remove their shoes; the doom of Korah, Dathan, and Abiram in Numbers 16:1–34; the destruction of Nadab and Abihu in Leviticus 10:1–3; and the punishment of King Uzziah in 2 Chronicles 26:16–21.

The truth that God is holy is the fundamental truth of the Bible—of the Old Testament and the New Testament—and of the Jewish religion and the

Christian religion. It is the preeminent factor in the Christian understanding of God. No fact in the Christian understanding of God needs to be more emphasized in our day than the fact of the absolute, unqualified, and uncompromising holiness of God. This is the chief note that is lacking in Christian Science, Theosophy, occultism, Buddhism, New Thought,* and all the base but boasted cults of the day. The great truth of God's holiness underlies the fundamental doctrines of the Bible—atonement by shed blood and justification by faith. The doctrine of the holiness of God is the keystone in the arch of Christian truth.

God Is Love

God is also love. This truth is declared in one of our texts for this chapter: *"God is love."* These words are found twice in the same chapter of the Bible (1 John 4:8, 16). This truth is essentially the same truth as *"God is light"* (1 John 1:5) and *"God is holy"* (Ps. 99:9), for the very essence of true holiness is love. Light is love, and love is light.

THE UNITY OF GOD

One more fact about the Christian understanding of God remains to be mentioned, and it is this: There is but one God. The unity of God comes out

---

* New Thought teaches that the power of the mind can achieve health and happiness. Its teachings are similar to those of Christian Science.

again and again in both the Old Testament and the New. For example, we read in Deuteronomy 4:35, *"The LORD Himself is God; there is none other besides Him."* And in Deuteronomy 6:4, we read, *"Hear, O Israel: the LORD our God, the LORD is one!"* Turning to the New Testament, we read, *"There is one God and one Mediator between God and men, the Man Christ Jesus"* (1 Tim. 2:5). And in Mark 12:29, our Lord Jesus Himself said, *"Hear, O Israel, the LORD our God, the LORD is one."*

But we must bear in mind the character of the divine unity. It is clearly revealed in the Bible that in this divine unity, in this one Godhead, there are three persons. This reality is expressed in a variety of ways.

In the first place, the Hebrew word translated *"one"* in the various passages given denotes a compound unity, not a simple unity. (See also John 17:22–23; 1 Corinthians 3:6–8; 1 Corinthians 12:13; and Galatians 3:28.)

In the second place, the Old Testament word most frequently used for God is a plural noun. The Hebrew grammarians and lexicographers tried to explain this by saying that it was the "pluralis majestatis" (*we* in place of *I* in the speech of royalty). But the very simple explanation is that the Hebrews, in spite of their intense monotheism, used a plural name for God because there is a plurality of persons in the one Godhead.

More striking yet, as a proof of the plurality of persons in the one Godhead, is the fact that God Himself uses plural pronouns in speaking of Himself. For example, in the first chapter of the Bible, we read that God said, *"Let Us make man in Our image, according to Our likeness"* (Gen. 1:26). And in Genesis 11:7, He is further recorded as saying, *"Come, let Us go down and there confuse their language, that they may not understand one another's speech."* In Genesis 3:22, we read, *"Then the LORD God said, 'Behold, the man has become like one of Us, to know good and evil.'"* And in that wonderful vision to which I have already referred, in which Isaiah saw Jehovah, we read this statement of Isaiah: *"Also I heard the voice of the Lord, saying: 'Whom shall I send, and who will go for Us?' Then I said, 'Here am I! Send me'"* (Isa. 6:8).

Another illustration of the plurality of persons in the one Godhead in the Old Testament understanding of God is found in Zechariah 2:10–11. Here Jehovah spoke of Himself as sent *by Jehovah* in these words:

> *"Sing and rejoice, O daughter of Zion! For behold, I am coming and I will dwell in your midst,"* says the LORD. *"Many nations shall be joined to the LORD in that day, and they shall become My people. And I will dwell in your midst. Then you will know that the LORD of hosts has sent Me to you."*

Here Jehovah clearly spoke of Himself as sent *by Jehovah*, thus clearly indicating two persons of the Deity.

This same thought of the plurality of persons in the one Godhead is brought out in John 1:1, where we reach the very climax of this thought. Here we are told, *"In the beginning was the Word, and the Word was with God, and the Word was God."* We will see later, when we come to study the deity of Christ and the personhood and deity of the Holy Spirit, that the Lord Jesus and the Holy Spirit are clearly designated as divine beings and, at the same time, are distinguished from one another and from God the Father. So it is clear that in the Christian understanding of God, while there is but one God, there are three persons in the one Godhead.

In these two chapters on the Christian understanding of God, I have inadequately stated this understanding. This understanding of God runs throughout the whole Bible, from the first chapter of the book of Genesis to the last chapter of the book of Revelation. This is one of the many marvelous illustrations of the divine unity of the Bible. How wonderful is that Book! There is unity of thought on this very profound doctrine pervading the whole Book! This is a clear indication that the Bible is the Word of God.

There is in the Bible a philosophy that is profounder than any human philosophy, ancient or modern. The only way to account for it is that God Himself is the author of this incomparable philosophy. What a wondrous God we have! How we ought to meditate on His person! With what awe and, at the same time, with what delight we should come into His presence and bow before Him, adoringly contemplating the wonder, beauty, majesty, and glory of His being.

Is Jesus Christ God?

4

Is Jesus Christ God?

While the Pharisees were gathered together,
Jesus asked them, saying, "What do you think
about the Christ? Whose Son is He?"
—Matthew 22:41–42

This question that our Lord Jesus asked the Pharisees is the most fundamental question concerning Christian thought and faith that can be asked of anybody in any age. Jesus Christ Himself is the center of Christianity, so the most fundamental questions of faith are those that concern the person of Christ. If a man holds right views concerning the person of Jesus Christ, he will sooner or later get right views on every other question. If he holds wrong views concerning the person of Jesus Christ, he is pretty sure to go wrong on everything else sooner or later. *"What do you think about the Christ?"* That is the great central question; that is the vital question.

The most fundamental question concerning the person of Christ is, Is Jesus Christ really God? Not merely, Is He divine? but, Is He actually God? When I was a boy, for a person to say that he believed in the divinity of Christ meant that he believed in the real deity of Christ, that he believed that Jesus is actually a divine person, that He is God. It no longer means that. The Devil is shrewd and subtle, and he knows that the most effective way to instill error into the minds of the uninformed and unwary is to take old and precious words and give them new meanings.

So when Satan's messengers, who masquerade as *"ministers of righteousness"* (2 Cor. 11:15), seek to lead, if possible, the elect astray (Matt. 24:24), they use the old precious words but with entirely new and entirely false meanings. They talk about "the divinity of Christ," but they do not mean at all by it what was meant in former days. In the same way, they talk about "the Atonement," but they do not mean at all by the Atonement the substitutionary death of Jesus Christ by which eternal life is secured for us. And often, when they talk about Christ, they do not mean at all our Lord and Savior Jesus Christ, the actual historical Jesus of the four gospels. They mean an "ideal Christ" or a "Christ principle."

Therefore, our subject in this chapter is not the divinity of Christ, but the deity of Christ. Our question is not, Is Jesus Christ divine? but, Is Jesus Christ God? Who was that person who was born at Bethlehem many centuries ago; who lived thirty-three or thirty-four years here on earth as recorded in the four gospels of Matthew, Mark, Luke, and John; who was crucified on Calvary's cross; who rose from the dead the third day; and who was exalted from earth to the right hand of the Father in heaven? Was He God manifested in the flesh? Was

He God embodied in a human being? Was He and is He a being worthy of our absolute faith, our supreme love, our unhesitating obedience, and our wholehearted worship, just as God the Father is worthy of our absolute faith, supreme love, unhesitating obedience, and wholehearted worship? Should all men honor Jesus Christ even as they honor God the Father (John 5:23)? The question is not merely whether He is an example that we can wisely follow or a master whom we can wisely serve, but whether He is a God whom we can rightly worship.

I presume that most of you, my readers, do believe that Jesus was God manifested in the flesh and that He is God today at the right hand of the Father. But why do you believe this? Are you so well-informed in your faith, and therefore so well-grounded, that no silver-tongued talker, no Unitarian* or Jehovah's Witness or Christian Scientist or Theosophist or other errorist, can confuse you and upset you and lead you astray? It is important that we be thoroughly sound in our faith on this point, and thoroughly well-informed, wherever else we may be in ignorance or error. For we are distinctly told in John 20:31 that *"these* [things] *are written that you may believe that Jesus is the Christ, the Son of God, and that believing you may have life in His name."* It is evident from these words of the inspired apostle John that this question is not merely a matter of theoretical opinion, but a matter that concerns our salvation. I am writing this chapter to strengthen

---

* Unitarianism denies the Christian doctrine of the Trinity and the Christian doctrine of the deity of Jesus Christ.

and instruct you in your blessed faith, your saving faith in Jesus Christ as a divine person.

When I studied the subject of the deity of Christ in a theological seminary, I got the impression that there are a few proof texts in the Bible that conclusively prove that He is God. Years later, I found that there are not merely a few proof texts that prove this fact, but that the Bible in many ways and in countless passages clearly teaches that Jesus Christ was God manifest in the flesh. Indeed, I found that the doctrine of the deity of Jesus Christ forms the very foundation of the Bible.

JESUS' DIVINE NAMES PROVE HIS DEITY

The first proof of the absolute deity of our Lord Jesus is that many names and titles clearly implying deity are used of Jesus Christ in the Bible, some of them repeatedly. In fact, the total number of passages reaches far into the hundreds. Of course, I can give you only a few illustrations. First of all, look at Revelation 1:17:

> *And when I saw Him* [Jesus], *I fell at His feet as dead. But He laid His right hand on me, saying to me, "Do not be afraid; I am the First and the Last."*

The context clearly shows that our Lord Jesus is the speaker, and here our Lord Jesus distinctly called Himself *"the First and the Last."* Now, beyond a question, this is a divine name, for we read in Isaiah 44:6,

Thus says the LORD, the King of Israel, and his Redeemer, the LORD of hosts: "I am the First and I am the Last; besides Me there is no God."

In Revelation 22:12–13, our Lord Jesus said that He is *"the Alpha and the Omega."* His words are,

Behold, I am coming quickly, and My reward is with Me, to give to every one according to his work. I am the Alpha and the Omega, the Beginning and the End, the First and the Last.

Now, in Revelation 1:8, *"the Lord God"* declared that *He* is *"the Alpha and the Omega."* His words are, *"I am the Alpha and the Omega, saith the Lord God, which is and which was and which is to come, the Almighty"* (RV).

In 1 Corinthians 2:8, the apostle Paul spoke of our crucified Lord Jesus as *"the Lord of glory."* His exact words are, *"Which none of the rulers of this age knew; for had they known, they would not have crucified the Lord of glory."* There can be no question that *"the Lord of glory"* is Jehovah God, for we read in Psalm 24:8–10,

Who is this King of glory? The LORD strong and mighty, the LORD mighty in battle. Lift up your heads, O you gates! Lift up, you everlasting doors! And the King of glory shall come in. Who is this King of glory? The LORD of hosts, He is the King of glory.

We are told in the passage already referred to that our crucified Lord Jesus is *"the Lord* [the King] *of glory"*; therefore, He must be Jehovah.

In John 20:28, Thomas addressed the Lord Jesus as his Lord and his God: *"And Thomas answered and said to Him, 'My Lord and my God!'"* Unitarians have endeavored to get around the force of this statement of Thomas by saying that Thomas was excited and that he was not addressing the Lord Jesus at all, but was saying, *"My Lord and my God!"* as an exclamation of astonishment, just in the way that the ungodly sometimes use these exclamations today. This interpretation is impossible, and it shows to what desperate measures the Unitarians are driven, for Jesus Himself commended Thomas for seeing the truth and saying it. Our Lord Jesus' words immediately following those of Thomas are, *"Thomas, because you have seen Me, you have believed. Blessed are those who have not seen and yet have believed"* (v. 29).

In Titus 2:13, our Lord Jesus is spoken of as *"God"*: *"Looking for the blessed hope and glorious appearing of our great God and Savior Jesus Christ."* In Romans 9:5, Paul told us that *"Christ...is over all, the eternally blessed God."* Unitarians have desperately tried to overcome the force of these words, but the only fair translation and interpretation of the words that Paul wrote in Greek are the translation and interpretation just given.

To the person who goes to the Bible to find out what it actually teaches—not to read his own thoughts into it—there can be no honest doubt that Jesus is spoken of by various names and titles that beyond a question imply deity, and that He is in so many words called God. In Hebrews 1:8, it is said of the Son, *"But to the Son He [God] says: 'Your throne, O God, is forever and ever; a scepter of righteousness is the scepter of Your Kingdom.'"* If we were to go no further, it is clearly the plain and often repeated teaching of the Bible that Jesus Christ is truly God.

JESUS' DIVINE ATTRIBUTES PROVE HIS DEITY

But there is a second proof that Jesus Christ is God, one that is equally convincing. It is this: all the distinctively divine attributes are ascribed to Jesus Christ, and in Him is said to dwell *"all the fullness of the Godhead"* (Col. 2:9). There are five distinctively divine attributes, that is, five attributes that God alone possesses. These are omnipotence, omniscience, omnipresence, eternity, and immutability. Each one of these distinctively divine attributes is ascribed to Jesus Christ.

First of all, omnipotence is ascribed to Jesus Christ. We are taught that Jesus had power over disease, death, winds, the sea, and demons; they were all subject to His word. In fact, He is *"far above all principality and power and might and dominion, and every name that is named, not only in this age but also in that which is to come"* (Eph. 1:21). In addition, the Bible says that He upholds *"all things by the word of His power"* (Heb. 1:3).

Omniscience is also ascribed to Jesus Christ. We are taught in the Bible that Jesus knew men's lives, even their secret histories (see John 4:16–19), that He knew the secret thoughts of men, knew all men, knew what was in man (Mark 2:8; Luke 5:22; John 2:24–25). Significantly, we are distinctly told in 2 Chronicles 6:30 and Jeremiah 17:9–10 that only God possesses this knowledge. In addition, we are told in so many words in John 16:30 that Jesus knew *"all things,"* and in Colossians 2:3 that in Him *"are hidden all the treasures of wisdom and knowledge."*

Omnipresence is also ascribed to Jesus Christ. We read in Matthew 18:20 that *"where two or three are gathered together in* [His] *name,"* He is *"in the midst of them."* And in Matthew 28:20, we are told that wherever His obedient disciples would go, He would be with them, *"even to the end of the age."* In John 14:20 and 2 Corinthians 13:5, we see that He dwells in each believer, in all the millions of believers scattered over the earth. In Ephesians 1:23, we are told that He *"fills all in all."*

Eternity is also ascribed to Jesus Christ. John 1:1 states that *"in the beginning was the Word, and the Word was with God, and the Word was God."* In John 8:58, Jesus Himself said, *"Most assuredly, I say to you, before Abraham was, I AM."* Note that the Lord Jesus did not merely say that "before Abraham was, I *was,"* but *"before Abraham was, I AM,"* thus declaring Himself to be the eternal *"I AM."* (See Exodus 3:14.) Even in the Old Testament, we have a declaration of the eternity of the Christ who was to be born in Bethlehem. In Micah 5:2, we read,

> *But you, Bethlehem Ephrathah, though you are little among the thousands of Judah, yet out of you shall come forth to Me the One to be Ruler in Israel, whose goings forth are from of old, from everlasting.*

And in Isaiah 9:6, we learn of the Child who was to be born,

> *Unto us a Child is born, unto us a Son is given; and the government will be upon His shoulder. And His name will be called Wonderful, Counselor, Mighty God, Everlasting Father, Prince of Peace.*

In Hebrews 13:8, we are told that *"Jesus Christ is the same yesterday, today, and forever."*

His immutability is also taught in the passage just quoted from Hebrews. In addition, in Hebrews 1:11–12, we see that while even the heavens change, the Lord Jesus does not change. The exact words are,

> *They* [the heavens] *will perish, but You remain; and they will all grow old like a garment; like a cloak You will fold them up, and they will be changed. But You are the same, and Your years will not fail.*

So we see that each one of the five distinctly divine attributes is ascribed to our Lord Jesus Christ. And in Colossians 2:9, we are told, *"In Him dwells all the fullness of the Godhead bodily"* (that is, in a bodily form). Here, again, we might rest our case, for what has been said about His divine attributes, even if taken alone, clearly proves the absolute deity of our Lord Jesus Christ. It shows that He possesses every perfection of nature and character that God the Father possesses.

JESUS' DIVINE OFFICES PROVE HIS DEITY

But we do not need to rest the case here. There is a third indisputable proof that Jesus Christ is God; namely, all the distinctively divine offices are attributed to Jesus Christ. The seven distinctively divine offices—seven things that God alone can do—are creation, preservation, forgiveness of sin, the raising of the dead, the transformation of bodies, judgment, and the bestowal of eternal life. Each of these distinctly divine offices is ascribed to Jesus Christ.

Creation is ascribed to Him. In Hebrews 1:10, these words are spoken to our Lord: *"You, LORD, in the beginning laid the foundation of the earth, and the heavens are the work of Your hands."* The context clearly shows that the Lord addressed here is the Lord Jesus. In John 1:3, we are told that *"all things were made through Him* [Jesus Christ], *and without Him nothing was made that was made."*

Preservation of the universe and of everything in it is also ascribed to Him in Hebrews 1:3, where it is said of the Lord Jesus,

> *Who being the brightness of His* [God's] *glory and the express image of His* [God's] *person, and **upholding all things by the word of His power**, when He had by Himself purged our sins, sat down at the right hand of the Majesty on high.* (emphasis added)

The forgiveness of sin is ascribed to Jesus Christ as well. Jesus Himself said in Mark 2:10, when His power to forgive sins was questioned because that was recognized as a divine power, *"The Son of Man has power on earth to forgive sins."*

The future raising of the dead is distinctly ascribed to Him in John 6:39, 44, where Jesus said,

> *This is the will of the Father who sent Me, that of all He has given Me I should lose nothing, but should raise it up at the last day....No one can come to Me unless the Father who sent Me draws him; and I will raise him up at the last day.*

The transformation of our bodies is ascribed to Him in Philippians 3:20–21: *"The Lord Jesus Christ ...will transform our lowly body that it may be conformed to His glorious body."*

In 2 Timothy 4:1, judgment is ascribed to Him. We are told that He *"will judge the living and the dead."* Jesus Himself declared that He would be the judge of all mankind and emphasized the fact of the divine character of that office. In John 5:22–23, He said,

> *For the Father judges no one, but has committed all judgment to the Son, that all should honor the Son just as they honor the Father. He who does not honor the Son does not honor the Father who sent Him.*

The bestowal of eternal life is ascribed to Jesus Christ again and again. In John 10:28, He Himself said, *"I give them eternal life, and they shall never perish; neither shall anyone snatch them out of My hand."* And in John 17:1–2, Jesus said,

> *Father, the hour has come. Glorify Your Son, that Your Son also may glorify You, as You have given Him authority over all flesh, that He should give eternal life to as many as You have given Him.*

Here, then, we have the seven distinctively divine offices all attributed to Jesus Christ. This evidence alone would prove that He is God, and we could rest the case here. But there are even more proofs of His absolute deity.

A COMPARISON OF OLD TESTAMENT AND NEW TESTAMENT VERSES PROVES HIS DEITY

The fourth proof of the absolute deity of Jesus Christ is found in the fact that over and over again statements that in the Old Testament are made distinctly of Jehovah are taken in the New Testament to refer to Jesus Christ. Many illustrations could be given, but I will give only one illustration here. In Jeremiah 11:20, the prophet said,

> *O LORD of hosts, You who judge righteously, testing the mind and the heart, let me see Your vengeance on them, for to You I have revealed my cause.*

Here the prophet Jeremiah distinctly said that it is Jehovah of Hosts who *"judge[s]"* and *"test[s] the mind and the heart."* And in Jeremiah 17:10, the prophet represented Jehovah Himself as saying the same thing in these words: *"I, the LORD, search the heart, I test the mind, even to give every man according to his ways, according to the fruit of his doings."*

But in the New Testament, the Lord Jesus said, *"I am He who searches the minds and hearts. And I will give to each one of you according to your works"* (Rev. 2:23). We are distinctly told in the context that it is *"the Son of God"* (v. 18) who is speaking here. So Jesus claimed for Himself in the New Testament what Jehovah in the Old Testament said is true of Himself and of Himself alone.

In many other instances, statements that in the Old Testament are made distinctly of Jehovah are taken in the New Testament to refer to Jesus Christ. This is to say, Jesus Christ occupies the place in New Testament thought and doctrine that Jehovah occupies in Old Testament thought and doctrine.

THE NAMES OF THE FATHER AND THE SON COUPLED TOGETHER PROVE CHRIST'S DEITY

The fifth proof of the absolute deity of our Lord is found in the way in which the name of Jesus Christ is coupled with that of God the Father. In numerous passages, His name is coupled with the name of God the Father in a way in which it would be impossible to couple the name of any finite being with that of Deity. I will give only a few of the many illustrations that could be given.

A striking instance is in the words of our Lord Himself in John 14:23, where we read,

> *Jesus answered and said to him, "If anyone loves Me, he will keep My word; and My Father will love him, and We will come to him and make Our home with him."*

Here our Lord Jesus did not hesitate to couple Himself with the Father in such a way as to say *"We"*—that is, "God the Father and I"—*"will come...and make Our home with him."*

In John 14:1, Jesus said, *"Let not your heart be troubled; you believe in God, believe also in Me."* If Jesus Christ is not God, this is shocking blasphemy. There is absolutely no middle ground between admitting the deity of Jesus Christ and charging Christ with the most daring and appalling blasphemy of which any man in all history was ever guilty.

CHRIST'S ACCEPTANCE OF WORSHIP PROVES HIS DEITY

There is a sixth proof of the absolute deity of our Lord Jesus. The proofs already given have been decisive—each one of the five has been decisive—but this, if possible, is the most decisive of them all. It is this: we are taught that Jesus Christ should be worshiped as God, both by angels and men. In numerous places in the Gospels, we see Jesus Christ accepting without hesitation a worship that good men and angels declined with fear and that He Himself taught should be rendered only to God. (See Matthew 14:33; Matthew 28:9; and Luke 24:52. Compare Matthew 4:9–10; Acts 10:25–26; and Revelation 22:8–9.)

A curious and very misleading comment is made in the margin of the American Standard Revision on the meaning of the word translated *"worship"* in these passages. It says, "The Greek word translated 'worship' denotes an act of reverence, *whether paid to a creature* or to the Creator" (emphasis added). Now, this is true, but it is utterly misleading. While this word is used to denote an act of reverence paid to a creature by *idolaters,* our Lord Jesus Himself distinctly said, using exactly the same Greek word, *"You shall worship the LORD your God, and Him only you shall serve"* (Matt. 4:10).

Furthermore, Jesus said in John 5:23 that *"all should honor the Son just as they honor the Father."* And in Revelation 5:8–9, 12–13, the four living creatures and the twenty-four elders are shown falling down before the Lamb and offering worship to Him just as worship is offered to Him who sits on the throne, that is, God the Father. In Hebrews 1:6, we are told, *"When He [God] again brings the firstborn [Jesus] into the world, He says: 'Let all the angels of God worship Him.'"*

One night, in a church in Chicago, I stepped up to an intelligent-looking man and asked him, "Are you a Christian?" He replied, "I do not suppose you would consider me a Christian." "Why not?" I asked. He said, "I am a Unitarian." I said, "What you mean, then, is that you do not think that Jesus Christ is a person who should be worshiped." He replied, "That is exactly what I think," and added, "The Bible nowhere says we ought to worship Him." I said, "Who told you that?" He replied, "My pastor," mentioning a prominent Unitarian minister in the city of Boston. I said, "Let me show you something," and I opened my Bible to Hebrews 1:6 and read, *"When He*

[God] *again brings the firstborn* [Jesus] *into the world, He says: 'Let all the angels of God worship Him.'"*

The Unitarian man said, "Does it say that?" I handed him the Bible and said, "Read it for yourself." He read it and said, "I did not know that was in the Bible." I said, "Well, it is there, isn't it?" "Yes, it is there." Language could not make it any plainer. The Bible clearly teaches that Jesus, the Son of God, is to be worshiped as God by angels and men, even as God the Father is worshiped.

ADDITIONAL VERSES AMAZINGLY PROVE CHRIST'S DEITY

The six proofs of the deity of Jesus Christ that I have given leave no possibility of doubting that Jesus Christ is God, that Jesus of Nazareth is God manifest in a human person, that He is a being to be worshiped, even as God the Father is worshiped. But there are also incidental proofs of His absolute deity that, if possible, are in some ways even more convincing than the direct assertions of His deity.

First, our Lord Jesus said in Matthew 11:28, *"Come to Me, all you who labor and are heavy laden, and I will give you rest."* Now, anyone who makes a promise like that must either be God, a lunatic, or an impostor. No one can give rest to all the weary and burdened who come to him unless he is God, yet Jesus Christ offers to do it. If He offers to do it and fails to do it when men come to Him, then He is either a lunatic or an impostor. If He actually does it, then beyond a question He is God. And thousands can testify that He actually does it. Thousands and tens of thousands who were weary and burdened and crushed, and for whom there was no help in man, have come to Jesus Christ, and He has given them rest. Surely, then, He is not merely a great man—He is God.

Second, in John 14:1, Jesus Christ demanded that we put the same faith in Him that we put in God the Father, and He promised that in such faith we will find a cure for all troubles and anxieties. His words are, *"Let not your heart be troubled; you believe in God, believe also in Me."* It is clear that He demanded that the same absolute faith be put in Him that is to be put in God Almighty. Now, in Jeremiah 17:5, a Scripture with which our Lord Jesus was perfectly familiar, we read, *"Thus says the LORD: 'Cursed is the man who trusts in man.'"* Yet regardless of this clear curse pronounced upon all who trust in man, Jesus Christ demanded that we put trust in Him just as we put trust in God. It is the strongest possible assertion of deity on His part. No one but God has a right to make such a demand, and Jesus Christ, when He made this demand, must either have been God or an impostor. Furthermore, thousands and tens of thousands have found that when they have believed in Him just as they believe in God, their hearts have been delivered from trouble no matter what their bereavement or circumstances have been.

Third, the Lord Jesus demanded supreme and absolute love for Himself. It is as clear as day that no one but God has a right to demand such a love, but there can be no question that Jesus did demand it.

In Matthew 10:37, He said to His disciples, *"He who loves father or mother more than Me is not worthy of Me. And he who loves son or daughter more than Me is not worthy of Me."* And in Luke 14:26, 33, He said,

> *If anyone comes to Me and does not hate his father and mother, wife and children, brothers and sisters, yes, and his own life also, he cannot be My disciple....So likewise, whoever of you does not forsake all that he has cannot be My disciple.*

There can be no question that this is a demand on Jesus' part of supreme and absolute love for Himself, a love that puts even the dearest loved ones in an entirely secondary place. No one but God has a right to make such a demand, but our Lord Jesus made it; therefore, He is God.

Fourth, the Lord Jesus claimed absolute equality with the Father. He said, *"I and My Father are one"* (John 10:30).

Fifth, our Lord Jesus went so far as to say, *"He who has seen Me has seen the Father"* (John 14:9). He claimed here to be so absolutely God that to see Him is to see the Father who dwells in Him.

Sixth, Jesus said, *"And this is eternal life, that they may know You, the only true God, and Jesus Christ whom You have sent"* (John 17:3). In other words, He claimed that knowledge of Himself is as essential a part of eternal life as knowledge of God the Father.

CHRIST'S DEITY: A GLORIOUS TRUTH

There is no room left to doubt the absolute deity of Jesus Christ. It is a glorious truth. The Savior in whom we believe is God—a Savior for whom nothing is too hard, a Savior who can save *from* the uttermost and *to* the uttermost (Heb. 7:25). Oh, how we should rejoice that we have no merely human Savior, but a Savior who is absolutely God.

On the other hand, how black is the guilt of rejecting such a Savior as this! Whoever refuses to accept Jesus as his divine Savior and Lord is guilty of the enormous sin of rejecting a Savior who is God. Many a man thinks he is good because he has never stolen or committed murder or cheated. "Of what great sin am I guilty?" he complacently asks. Have you ever accepted Jesus Christ? "No." Well, then, you are guilty of the awful and damning sin of rejecting a Savior who is God. "But," he answers, "I do not believe that He is God." That does not change the fact or lessen your guilt. Questioning a fact or denying a fact never changes it, regardless of what anyone may say to the contrary.

Suppose a man has a wife who is one of the noblest, purest, truest women who has ever lived. Would her husband's bringing baseless charges against her, questioning her purity and loyalty, change the fact? It would not. It would simply make that husband guilty of awful slander; it would simply prove that man to be an outrageous scoundrel. Likewise, denying the deity of Jesus Christ does not make His deity any less a fact, but it does make the denier of His deity guilty of awful, incredible, blasphemous slander.

Is Jesus Christ
Truly Man?

5

Is Jesus Christ Truly Man?

*And the Word [Jesus Christ] became flesh and
dwelt among us, and we beheld His glory,
the glory as of the only begotten of the
Father, full of grace and truth.*
—John 1:14

*[Jesus], being in the form of God, did not consider it
robbery to be equal with God, but made Himself of no
reputation, taking the form of a bondservant, and
coming in the likeness of men. And being found in
appearance as a man, He humbled Himself and
became obedient to the point of death,
even the death of the cross.*
—Philippians 2:6–8

*There is one God and one Mediator between God
and men, the Man Christ Jesus.*
—1 Timothy 2:5

I n the preceding chapter, we saw many things
about Jesus Christ. First, we saw that *"in Him
dwells all the fullness of the Godhead bodily"*
(Col. 2:9). He possesses all the distinctively divine

attributes and exercises all the distinctively divine offices. He occupies the position in New Testament thought that Jehovah occupies in Old Testament thought. He is a being worthy of our absolute faith, supreme love, unhesitating obedience, and whole-hearted worship. In summary, we saw that He was God and is God.

But in this chapter's three texts, we are told that this Divine One, who had existed from all eternity with God the Father and who was God, became a man. In becoming a man, He did not cease to be God; however, the Word, the Eternal Word, which was *"with God"* and *"was God"* (John 1:1), took human nature upon Himself. While Jesus was very God of very God, He was also a real man, as truly and completely a man as any man who has ever walked on this earth.

The doctrine of the real humanity of Christ is as essential a part of the Christian faith as the doctrine of His real deity. There is a very large group of people who do not accept the real deity of Jesus Christ. They are in fundamental error. Another large group of people accept only His deity and do not accept the reality of His humanity. They also are in error. A doctrine of a Savior who is only man is a false doctrine, and a doctrine of a Savior who is only God is an equally false doctrine. The doctrine of the Bible is that One who from all eternity was God became man in the person of Jesus of Nazareth. There are many passages in the Bible that set forth the deity of our Lord Jesus in a way that is unmistakable and inescapable. Many other passages in the Bible set forth the complete humanity of our Lord Jesus in a way that is equally unmistakable and inescapable. It is with the doctrine of His real humanity that we are concerned in this chapter.

THE HUMAN PARENTAGE OF JESUS CHRIST

First of all, the Bible teaches that Jesus Christ had a human parentage. We read in Luke 2:7,

> *And she* [Mary] *brought forth her firstborn Son, and wrapped Him in swaddling cloths, and laid Him in a manger, because there was no room for them in the inn.*

Here we are told that our Lord Jesus Christ, though supernaturally conceived, was Mary's son. Mary was as truly His mother as God was His Father. He had a human parentage as truly as He had a divine parentage.

In Luke 1:35, we read,

> *And the angel answered and said to her* [Mary], *"The Holy Spirit will come upon you, and the power of the Highest will overshadow you; therefore, also, that Holy One who is to be born will be called the Son of God."*

He was called *"the Son of God"* because He was begotten directly by the power of the Holy Spirit. But the Holy Spirit came upon Mary, and she became the mother of this One who was to be called *"the Son of God."*

Jesus' human parentage was not only reflected in the fact that He descended from Mary; we are also clearly told in Romans 1:3 that God's Son *"was born of the seed of David according to the flesh."* In Acts 2:30, we are told that He was *"the fruit of his [David's] body, according to the flesh."* And in Hebrews 7:14, we are told that *"our Lord arose from Judah."* While we read in Galatians 4:4 that *"when the fullness of the time had come, God sent forth His Son,"* we are also told with equal plainness in the same verse that this Son of God was *"born of a woman."* The human parentage of our Lord and Savior Jesus Christ is just as real and just as essential a part of Him as His divine parentage.

THE HUMAN PHYSICAL NATURE OF
JESUS CHRIST

Not only did Jesus Christ have a human parentage, but He had a human physical nature, a human body. This comes out in the first of our texts: *"The Word became flesh"* (John 1:14). In Hebrews 2:14, we are taught that

> *inasmuch then as the children have partaken of flesh and blood, He [our Lord Jesus] Himself likewise shared in the same, that through death He might destroy him who had the power of death, that is, the devil.*

Words could not make it any plainer that our Lord Jesus had a real human body, a real human physical nature. Indeed, the apostle John taught us that not to believe in the actuality of His human body is a mark of the Antichrist. He said,

By this you know the Spirit of God: Every spirit that confesses that Jesus Christ has come in the flesh is of God, and every spirit that does not confess that Jesus Christ has come in the flesh is not of God. And this is the spirit of the Antichrist, which you have heard was coming, and is now already in the world.

(1 John 4:2–3)

There were those in John's day who denied the reality of Jesus' human nature, who asserted that His body was only a seeming or apparent body, that it was an illusion, or, as the Christian Scientists now put it, "mortal thought." John, speaking in the wisdom and power of the Holy Spirit, asserted that this doctrine is a mark of the Antichrist. It is the one supreme mark today that Christian Science is of the Antichrist.

Not only did Jesus Christ have a human body during His life here on earth, but He still had a human body after His resurrection. The Millennial Dawnists* tell us that this is not so. They say that before His incarnation He was wholly a spiritual being, at His incarnation He became wholly a human being, and after His death and resurrection He became wholly a divine being. All of this is unscriptural and is therefore untrue. Jesus Himself said to His disciples after His resurrection,

"Behold My hands and My feet, that it is I Myself. Handle Me and see, for a spirit does not

---

* Also known as the Dawn Bible Students, this cult sprang from the teachings of Charles Taze Russell, whose teachings also led to the formation of the cult known as the Jehovah's Witnesses.

*have flesh and bones as you see I have." When
He had said this, He showed them His hands
and His feet.   (Luke 24:39–40)*

And Jesus said to Thomas, after Thomas had
doubted the reality of His resurrection, *"Reach your
finger here, and look at My hands; and reach your
hand here, and put it into My side. Do not be unbe-
lieving, but believing"* (John 20:27).

Not only did Jesus have a real human body after
His resurrection while He was still here on earth,
but He retains His human body in heaven. Of that
wonderful view into heaven that was given to Stephen at the time he was stoned and killed, we read,

*But he, being full of the Holy Spirit, gazed into
heaven and saw the glory of God, and Jesus
standing at the right hand of God, and said,
"Look! I see the heavens opened and the Son of
Man standing at the right hand of God!"*
(Acts 7:55–56)

Furthermore, when Christ comes again to take
His rightful authority on this earth, He will come
with a human body. He will come as *"the Son of
Man."* He Himself said to the high priest when He
stood before him on trial, *"Hereafter you will see the
Son of Man sitting at the right hand of the Power,
and coming on the clouds of heaven"* (Matt. 26:64).
In these words of our Lord, we have both a clear
declaration of His deity and an equally clear declaration that He was a real man and will come again
as a real man with a human, though glorified, body.

Indeed, we are told in Philippians 3:20–21 that when He does come in this way, He is going to transform our present human bodies into the likeness of His own *"glorious body"* (v. 21)—His glorified human body.

THE HUMAN LIMITATIONS OF JESUS CHRIST

The reality and completeness of our Lord's human nature come out in the fact that He had a human parentage and a human body, but that is not all. We are also clearly taught that, while as God He possessed all the attributes and exercised all the offices of Deity, as a man He was subject to human limitations.

His Physical Limitations

Jesus was subject to the physical limitations that are inherent to humanity. In John 4:6, we read that Jesus Christ was weary. The words are, *"Jesus therefore, being wearied from His journey, sat thus by the well. It was about the sixth hour."* But God is never weary. We read explicitly in Isaiah 40:28,

Have you not known? Have you not heard? The everlasting God, the LORD, the Creator of the ends of the earth, neither faints nor is weary.

We are told in Matthew 8:24 that Jesus Christ slept. But God never sleeps. Psalm 121:4–5 says, *"Behold, He who keeps Israel shall neither slumber* nor sleep. *The* LORD *is your keeper; the* LORD *is your shade at your right hand."* By comparing these two verses, we see distinctly that Jehovah never sleeps, yet Jesus did sleep. So Jesus was Jehovah, but He was not Jehovah only. He was man as truly as He was God.

In Matthew 21:18 and John 19:28, we read that Jesus Christ was hungry and thirsty. In Luke 22:44, we see that Jesus Christ suffered physical agony. His agony was so great that He was on the point of dying with agony.

In 1 Corinthians 15:3, we read that Christ died. First Corinthians 15:1–3 reveals that Jesus' death is an essential part of the Gospel. Paul said,

> *Moreover, brethren, I declare to you the gospel which I preached to you, which also you received and in which you stand, by which also you are saved, if you hold fast that word which I preached to you; unless you believed in vain. For I delivered to you first of all that which I also received: that Christ died for our sins according to the Scriptures.*

Christ's death was not merely an "apparent" death; it was a real death. It was no illusion. Our salvation depends on the reality of His death.

Christian Science cuts the very heart out of the Gospel by denying the reality of His death. I am often asked, "Was it the human nature of Jesus Christ that died, or was it the divine nature that died?" It was neither the one nor the other. Natures do not die; persons die. It was *Jesus* who died, the Person who was at once God and man. We are told in 1 Corinthians 2:8 that they *"crucified the Lord of glory,"* and we saw in the last chapter that *"the Lord of glory"* is unquestionably a divine title. It was the one person Jesus, at once human and divine, who died on the cross of Calvary.

His Intellectual and Moral Limitations

Jesus Christ was also, as a man, subject to intellectual and moral limitations. We read in Luke 2:52, *"Jesus increased in wisdom and stature, and in favor with God and men."* Since we are told here that He grew in wisdom, He must have been more perfect in wisdom after He grew than before He grew. And since He grew in favor with God and man, He must have attained to a higher type of moral perfection when He grew than He had attained to before He grew. God was incarnate in the Babe of Bethlehem; nevertheless, Jesus was a real babe and grew not only in stature, but in wisdom and in favor with God and man.

As a man, Jesus was limited in knowledge. He Himself said in Mark 13:32,

> But of that day and hour [that is, the day and the hour of His own return] *no one knows, not even the angels in heaven, nor the Son, but only the Father.*

Of course, His knowledge was *self-limited*. To set an example for you and me to follow, He voluntarily *as a man* put away His knowledge of the time of His own return.

Furthermore, we are definitely and explicitly taught in Hebrews 4:15 that Jesus Christ was *"in all points tempted as we are."* We should bear in mind that this is a clear and complete proof of the reality of His humanity—not only physical but mental and moral. We should also bear in mind what is stated in the same verse, that He was *"without sin"*; that is, there was not the slightest taint or tinge of sin in His temptations, not one moment's yielding to them in thought or desire or act. He was tempted and overcame temptation in the same way that we may overcome it—by the Word of God and prayer. He Himself voluntarily placed Himself under the basic moral limitations that man is under, in order to redeem man.

His Limitations in Obtaining and Exercising Power

As a man, Jesus was also subject to limitations in the ways in which He obtained power and exercised power. Jesus Christ obtained power for the divine work that He did while here on earth, not by His incarnate deity, but by prayer. We read in Mark 1:35, *"Now in the morning, having risen a long while before daylight, He went out and departed to a solitary place; and there He prayed."* And we read also that before He raised Lazarus from the dead— before He called him forth from the tomb by His word—He lifted up His eyes to God and said, *"Father, I thank You that You have heard Me"* (John 11:41). By this He showed conclusively that the power by which He raised Lazarus from the dead was not His inherent, inborn, divine power, but was power obtained by prayer. It is mentioned not less than twenty-five times in the New Testament that Jesus prayed. He obtained power for work and for moral victory as other men do—by prayer.

Again, Jesus was subject to human conditions for obtaining what He desired. He obtained power for the divine works and miracles that he did by the anointing of the Holy Spirit as well as by prayer. We read in Acts 10:38,

> *God anointed Jesus of Nazareth with the Holy Spirit and with power, who went about doing good and healing all who were oppressed by the devil, for God was with Him.*

We are taught, furthermore, that Jesus was subject, during His earthly life, to limitations in the exercise of power. He Himself said just before His crucifixion and subsequent glorification,

> *Most assuredly, I say to you, he who believes in Me, the works that I do he will do also; and greater works than these he will do, because I go to My Father.*   *(John 14:12)*

The evident meaning of this Scripture is that during the days of His earthly existence there was a limitation to His exercise of power. But then He was glorified with the Father with the glory that He had with Him before the world was (John 17:5). After His glorification, there were no more limitations to the exercise of His power. Therefore, we, being united to our Lord Jesus, not as He was on earth but as He is in His exaltation and restoration to divine glory, will do greater works than He did during the days of His earthly existence.

THE HUMAN RELATIONSHIP THAT JESUS HAD WITH GOD

The completeness of the humanity of Jesus Christ comes out in still another matter, that is, the relationship that He had with God. God was His God. He Himself said to Mary in John 20:17,

> *Do not cling to Me, for I have not yet ascended to My Father; but go to My brethren and say to them, "I am ascending to My Father and your Father, and to My God and your God."*

The evident meaning of this verse is that Jesus Christ's relationship to God the Father was the relationship between a man and God. He spoke of God the Father as *"My God."* Though possessing all the attributes and exercising all the functions of Deity, Jesus Christ the Son was subordinate to the Father.

This truth explains statements of our Lord that have puzzled many who believe in His deity. One example of a puzzling statement is in John 14:28, where Jesus said,

> *You have heard Me say to you, "I am going away and coming back to you." If you loved Me, you would rejoice because I said, "I am going to the Father," for My Father is greater than I.*

The question is often asked, "If Jesus Christ is God, how could the Father be greater than He?" The very simple answer to this is that He, *as the Son,* is subordinate to the Father. He is equal to the Father in the possession of all the distinctively divine attributes, in the exercise of all the divine offices, and as an object of our wholehearted worship, but He is subordinate to the Father in His position as Son. Jesus Christ's relationship to the Father is like the relationship of the wife to the husband in this respect. The wife may be fully the equal of the husband; nevertheless, *"the head of woman is man"* (1 Cor. 11:3). This means that she is subordinate to the man. We are told in the same verse that *"the head of Christ is God."* This means that Jesus Christ the Son is subordinate to the Father.

JESUS CHRIST: A REAL MAN IN EVERY WAY

It is evident from what we have read from God's Word that Jesus Christ in every respect was a true man, a real man, a complete man. He was made *"in all things...like His brethren"* (Heb. 2:17). He was subject to all the physical, mental, and moral conditions of existence inherent to human nature. He was in every respect a real man. He became this way voluntarily in order to redeem men. From all eternity He had existed *"in the form of God"* (Phil. 2:6) and could have remained *"in the form of God,"* but if He had remained that way, we would have been lost. Therefore, out of love for us, the fallen race, He

did not consider it robbery to be equal with God, but made Himself of no reputation, taking the

*form of a bondservant, and coming in the like-
ness of men. And being found in appearance
as a man, He humbled Himself and became
obedient to the point of death, even the death of
the cross.* (Phil. 2:6–8)

Oh, wondrous love! Out of love for us, He took
our nature upon Himself, turning His back on the
glory that had been His from all eternity. He took
upon Himself all the shame and suffering that was
involved in our redemption and became one of us so
that He could die for us and redeem us. Oh, the
wondrous grace of our Lord Jesus Christ! *"Though
He was rich, yet for your sakes He became poor, that
you through His poverty might become rich"* (2 Cor.
8:9). He partook of human nature so that we might
become partakers of the divine nature (2 Pet. 1:4).
The philosophy of the divine and human natures of
Christ, which is the philosophy of the New Testament, is a most wonderful philosophy—the most
wonderful philosophy the world has ever heard. And,
thank God, it is true.

RECONCILING TWO APPARENTLY
CONTRADICTORY DOCTRINES

Someone may ask, "How can we reconcile the
biblical doctrine of the true deity of Jesus Christ
with the biblical doctrine of the true humanity of
Jesus Christ? How can we reconcile the doctrine that
He was truly God with the doctrine that He was
equally truly man?" The answer to this question is
very simple. Reconciling doctrines is not our main

business. Our first business is to find out what the various passages in the Bible mean, taken in their natural, grammatical interpretation. Then, if we can reconcile them, well and good. If not, we should still believe them. We should leave the reconciliation of the two apparently conflicting doctrines to our increasing knowledge, as we go on communing with God and studying His Word. It is an utterly foolish and wrong idea that we must interpret every passage of the Bible in such a way that we can readily reconcile it with every other passage. It is this idea of interpretation that gives rise to one-sided, and therefore untrue, theology.

One man, for example, takes the passages in the Bible concerning the sovereignty of God, which Calvinists emphasize, and believes them. Then he twists and distorts the other passages that teach the freedom of man to make them fit with those that teach the sovereignty of God. In this way, he becomes a one-sided Calvinist. Another man sees only the passages that clearly teach man's power of self-determination, which Arminians emphasize. Then he seeks to twist all the passages that teach the sovereignty of God and the foreordaining wisdom and will of God. In this way, he becomes a one-sided Arminian. And so it is with the whole gamut of doctrine.

It is utter foolishness, to say nothing of presumption, to thus handle the Word of God deceitfully. Our business is to find out the plainly intended sense of a passage that we are studying, as determined by the usage of words, grammatical construction, and context. When we have discovered the plainly intended meaning, we are to believe it whether we can reconcile it with something else that we have found out and believe or not.

Two truths that seem to be utterly irreconcilable or flatly contradictory often, with increased knowledge, are seen to beautifully harmonize. We should always remember this point. Then we will have no difficulty in recognizing the fact that truths that still seem to be contradictory to us do perfectly harmonize in the infinite wisdom of God. Moreover, they will perfectly harmonize in our minds when we more closely approach God's omniscience.

SETTING CHRIST'S DEITY AND HIS HUMANITY SIDE BY SIDE

The Bible, in the most fearless way, puts the absolute deity of Jesus Christ in closest juxtaposition with the true humanity of Jesus Christ. For example, we read in Matthew 8:24, *"And suddenly a great tempest arose on the sea, so that the boat was covered with the waves. But He* [Jesus] *was asleep."* Here we have a plain statement of the real humanity of our Lord. But two verses later, in the twenty-sixth verse, we read,

> But He said to them, "Why are you fearful, O you of little faith?" Then He arose and rebuked the winds and the sea, and there was a great calm.

Here we have a clear shining forth of His deity, even the winds and the waves being subject to His word. No wonder the disciples asked one another, *"Who*

can this be, that even the winds and the sea obey
Him?" (v. 27). The answer is plain: a divine Man.

Again, we read in Luke 3:21, *"When all the people were baptized, it came to pass that Jesus also was
baptized; and while He prayed, the heaven was
opened."* Here we see Jesus in His humanity, baptized and praying. Surely this is a man. But in the
next verse we read,

> And the Holy Spirit descended in bodily form
> like a dove upon Him, and a voice came from
> heaven which said, "You are My beloved Son;
> in You I am well pleased."

Here, with an audible voice, God declared Him to be
divine, to be His Son.

In John 11:38 we read, *"Then Jesus, again
groaning in Himself, came to the tomb. It was a cave,
and a stone lay against it."* Here we see Jesus in His
humanity, but five verses further down, we read,
*"Now when He had said these things, He cried with
a loud voice, 'Lazarus, come forth!' And he who had
died came out"* (vv. 43–44). Here His deity shines
forth.

In Luke 9:28, we read, *"Now it came to pass,
about eight days after these sayings, that He took Peter, John, and James and went up on the mountain
to pray."* Here we very clearly see Jesus' humanity,
His limitation, His dependence on God. But in the
very next verse, we read, *"As He prayed, the appearance of His face was altered, and His robe became
white and glistening."* Here we see His divinity
shining forth. Then, again, in the thirty-fifth verse,
we read of the voice coming out of the cloud, saying,

"This is My beloved Son. Hear Him!" Jesus' deity is unmistakably revealed again.

In Matthew 16:16–17, we read,

> *Simon Peter answered and said, "You are the Christ, the Son of the living God." Jesus answered and said to him, "Blessed are you, Simon Bar-Jonah, for flesh and blood has not revealed this to you, but My Father who is in heaven."*

Here is a clear declaration by Jesus Himself of His deity. But four verses further down, we read,

> *From that time Jesus began to show to His disciples that He must go to Jerusalem, and suffer many things from the elders and chief priests and scribes, and be killed, and be raised the third day.*   *(Matt. 16:21)*

Here we have the clear declaration of the reality and completeness of His humanity.

In Hebrews 1:6, we read of our Lord Jesus, *"When He* [God the Father] *again brings the firstborn* [Jesus] *into the world, He says: 'Let all the angels of God worship Him.'"* Here is a most unmistakable and inescapable declaration that Jesus Christ is a divine person, to be worshiped as God by angels as well as by men. In verse 8, we read this further declaration of His absolute deity: *"But to the Son He* [God] *says: 'Your throne, O God, is forever and ever.'"* Here, again, the Son is declared to be God. But in the very next chapter, we read, *"For in that He Himself has suffered, being tempted, He is able to aid those who are tempted"* (Heb. 2:18). Here we have the clearest possible declaration of the reality of His human nature.

In Hebrews 4:14, we read, *"Seeing then that we have a great High Priest who has passed through the heavens, Jesus the Son of God, let us hold fast our confession."* Here we have a plain declaration of His deity. But in the very next verse, we read, *"For we do not have a High Priest who cannot sympathize with our weaknesses, but was in all points tempted as we are, yet without sin"*—one of the Bible's plainest declarations of the fullness and completeness of His humanity.

The doctrine of the deity of Jesus Christ and the doctrine of the humanity of Jesus Christ go hand in hand in the Bible. What kind of a Savior, what kind of a Lord Jesus, do you believe in? Do you believe in a Savior who is man and man only? Then you do not believe in the Savior who is presented in the Bible. On the other hand, do you believe in a Savior who is God and God only? Then you do not believe in the Savior of the Bible. The Lord Jesus, our Lord and Savior, presented to us in the Bible, is very God of very God and, at the same time, is our brother, our fellowman, and is not ashamed to call us brethren (Heb. 2:11).

Oh, I thank God that I have a Savior who is God, possessing all the attributes and powers of Deity, all the perfections of Deity—a Savior for whom nothing is too hard. I thank God that my Savior is One who made the heavens and the earth, and who holds all the powers of nature and of history in His control. But I equally thank God that my Savior is my brother man, One who was tempted in all points as I am (Heb. 4:15). I truly thank God that my Savior was in a position to bear my sins (Heb. 9:28), on the one hand because He is God, on the other hand because He is man. A merely divine Savior could not be a Savior for me. A merely human Savior could not be a Savior for me. But a Savior in whom Deity and humanity meet, a Savior who is at once God and man, is just the Savior I need, and just the Savior you need. He is a Savior who is *"able to save to the uttermost"* all who come to God through Him (Heb. 7:25).

Is the Holy Spirit
a Person?

6

Is the Holy Spirit a Person?

The communion of the Holy Spirit be with you.
—2 Corinthians 13:14

The doctrine of the personhood of the Holy Spirit is both fundamental and vital. Anyone who does not know the Holy Spirit as a person has not arrived at a complete and well-rounded Christian experience. Anyone who knows God the Father and God the Son but does not know God the Holy Spirit has not arrived at the Christian understanding of God. At first glance, it may seem to you that the doctrine of the personhood of the Holy Spirit is a purely technical and apparently impractical doctrine, but it is not. As we will see shortly, the doctrine of the personhood of the Holy Spirit is a doctrine of utmost practical importance.

THE IMPORTANCE OF THE DOCTRINE OF THE PERSONHOOD OF THE HOLY SPIRIT

From the Standpoint of Worship

This doctrine is vital from the standpoint of worship. If we do not know the Holy Spirit as a divine

117

person, if we think of Him as only an impersonal influence or power, then we are robbing a divine person of the worship that is His due, and the love that is His due, and the trust and surrender and obedience that are His due.

May I stop at this point to ask you, "Do you worship the Holy Spirit?" Theoretically, we all do, every time we sing the doxology,

> Praise God from whom all blessings flow,
> Praise Him all creatures here below.
> Praise Him above, ye heavenly hosts,
> Praise Father, Son, *and Holy Ghost.*

Theoretically, we all do, every time we sing the Gloria Patri: "Glory be to the Father and to the Son *and to the Holy Ghost,* as it was in the beginning, is now, and ever shall be, world without end. Amen." But it is one thing to do a thing theoretically and quite another thing to do it in actuality. It is one thing to sing words and quite another thing to realize the meaning and the force of the words that we sing.

I had a striking illustration of this some years ago. I was going to a Bible conference in New York State. I had to pass through a city four miles from the place where the conference was being held. A relative of mine lived in that city, and on the way to the conference I stopped to see my relative, who went with me to the conference. This relative was much older than I and had been a Christian much longer than I. She was a member of the Presbyterian Church and was thoroughly orthodox. That morning at the conference, I spoke on the personhood of the Holy Spirit. After the meeting was over, we were standing on the veranda of the hotel when she turned to me and said, "Archie, I never thought of *it* before as a person." Well, I had never thought of *it* as a person, but thank God I had come to know *Him* as a person.

From a Practical Standpoint

In the second place, it is of the highest importance from a practical standpoint that we know the Holy Spirit as a person. If you think of the Holy Spirit, as even so many Christians do, as a mere influence or power, then your thought will be, "How can I get hold of the Holy Spirit and use it?" But if you think of Him in the biblical way, as a divine person, your thought will be, "How can the Holy Spirit get hold of me and use me?" There is a great difference between man—the worm—using God to thresh the mountain, and God using man, the worm, to thresh the mountain. (See Isaiah 41:14–15.) The former concept is heathenish; essentially, it is no different from the concept of primitive tribes in Africa using magical charms and trying to control their gods. On the other hand, the concept of God the Holy Spirit getting hold of and using us is sublime and Christian.

Again, if you think of the Holy Spirit merely as an influence or power, your thought will be, "How can I get more of the Holy Spirit?" But if you think of Him in the biblical way as a person, your thought will be, "How can the Holy Spirit get more of me?"

The concept of the Holy Spirit as a mere influence or power inevitably leads to self-confidence, self-exaltation, and the parade of self. If you think of the Holy Spirit as an influence or power, and then fancy that you have received the Holy Spirit, the inevitable result will be that you will strut around as if you belonged to a superior order of Christians. I remember a woman who came to me one afternoon at the Northfield Bible Conference and said to me, "Brother Torrey, I want to ask you a question. But before I do, I want you to understand that I am a Holy Spirit woman." Her words made me shudder.

On the other hand, if you think of the Holy Spirit in the biblical way, as a divine person of infinite majesty who comes to dwell in our hearts and take possession of us and use us, you are led to self-renunciation, self-denial, and deep humility. I know of no thought that is more calculated to induce meekness than this great biblical truth about the Holy Spirit.

From the Standpoint of Experience

The doctrine of the personhood of the Holy Spirit is of the highest importance from the standpoint of experience. Thousands and tens of thousands of Christian men and women can testify to an entire transformation in their lives through coming to know the Holy Spirit as a person. In fact, this subject of the personhood of the Holy Spirit, which I have covered in almost every city in which I have held a series of meetings, is in some respects the deepest and most technical subject that I have ever attempted to handle before a public audience. Yet, notwithstanding that fact, more men and women have come to me or written to me at the close of the meetings, testifying to personal blessing received, than after covering any other subject that God has permitted me to speak on.

FOUR PROOFS OF THE PERSONHOOD OF THE HOLY SPIRIT

There are four separate and distinct proofs of the personhood of the Holy Spirit.

The Holy Spirit Has Characteristics That Only a Person Could Have

The first proof of the personhood of the Holy Spirit is that all the distinctive marks or characteristics of personhood are ascribed to the Holy Spirit in the Bible. What are the distinctive characteristics of personhood? Knowledge, will, and feeling. Any being who knows and wills and feels is a person. Often, when I say that the Holy Spirit is a person, people think that I mean that the Holy Spirit has hands and feet and fingers and toes and eyes and ears and so on. But these are not the marks of personhood; these are the marks of bodily existence. Any being who knows, wills, and feels is a person, whether he has a body or not. Now, all three characteristics of personhood are ascribed to the Holy Spirit in the Bible.

Knowledge

Read, for instance, 1 Corinthians 2:11:

For what man knows the things of a man except the spirit of the man which is in him? Even so no one knows the things of God except the Spirit of God.

Here knowledge is ascribed to the Holy Spirit. In other words, the Holy Spirit is not a mere illumination that comes to our minds whereby our minds are cleared and strengthened to see truth that they would not otherwise discover. The Holy Spirit is a person who Himself knows the things of God and reveals to us what He knows.

Will

We read in 1 Corinthians 12:11, *"But one and the same Spirit works all these things, distributing to each one individually as He wills."* In this verse, will is ascribed to the Holy Spirit. Clearly the thought is not that the Holy Spirit is a divine power that we get hold of and use according to our will, but that the Holy Spirit is a person who gets hold of us and uses us according to His will. This is one of the most fundamental facts about the Holy Spirit that we must bear in mind if we are to get into right relationship with Him.

More people are going astray at this point than almost any other. They are trying to acquire some divine power that they can use according to their own will. I thank God that there is no divine power that I can possess and use according to my will. What could I, in my foolishness and ignorance, do with a divine power? What evil I might work! On the other hand, I am even gladder that while there is no divine power that I can get hold of and use according to my foolish will, there is a divine person who can get hold of me and use me according to His infinitely wise and loving will.

Romans 8:27 tells us, *"Now He who searches the hearts knows what the mind of the Spirit is, because He makes intercession for the saints according to the will of God."* What I wish you to notice here is the expression *"the mind of the Spirit."* The Greek word here translated *"mind"* is a comprehensive word that has in it the ideas of both thought and purpose. It is the same word that is used in the seventh verse of the chapter, where we read, *"The carnal mind is enmity against God."* This does not mean merely that the thought of the flesh is against God, but that the whole moral and intellectual life of the flesh is against God.

Feeling

Now let us look at a most remarkable passage:

Now I beg you, brethren, through the Lord Jesus Christ, and through the love of the Spirit, that you strive together with me in prayers to God for me. (Rom. 15:30)

What I wish you to notice in this verse are the words *"the love of the Spirit."* That the Holy Spirit loves us is a wonderful thought. It teaches us that the Holy Spirit is not a mere blind influence or power that comes into our hearts and lives. He is a divine person, loving us with the tenderest love.

I wonder how many believers have ever thought much about *"the love of the Spirit."* I wonder how many ministers have ever preached a sermon on *"the love of the Spirit."* Every day of your life you kneel down before God the Father, at least I hope you do, and say, "Heavenly Father, I thank You for Your great love that led You to give Your Son to come down to this world and die on the cross of Calvary in my place." Every day of your life you kneel down before Jesus Christ the Son and say, "Blessed Son of God, I thank You for that great love of Yours that led You to come down to this world in obedience to the Father and die in my place on the cross of Calvary." But have you ever knelt down and looked to the Holy Spirit and said to Him, "Holy Spirit, I thank You for that great love of Yours"?

We owe our salvation as much to the love of the Holy Spirit as we do to the love of the Father and of the Son. If it had not been for the love of God the Father looking down on me in my lost state, yes, anticipating my fall and ruin and sending His Son down to this world to die on the cross, to die in my place, I would be in hell today. If it had not been for the love of Jesus Christ the Son, who came down to this world in obedience to the Father to lay down His life, who was a perfect atoning sacrifice on the cross of Cavalry in my place, I would be in hell today. But if it had not been for the love of the Holy Spirit, who came down to this world in obedience to the Father and the Son and sought me out in my lost condition, I would be in hell today.

The Holy Spirit continued to follow me when I would not listen to Him, when I deliberately turned my back on Him, when I insulted Him. He followed me into places where it must have been agony for One so holy to go. He followed me day after day, week after week, month after month, year after year, until at last He succeeded in bringing me to my senses. He brought me to realize my utterly lost condition and revealed the Lord Jesus to me as just the Savior I needed. He induced me and enabled me to receive the Lord Jesus as my Savior and my Lord. I repeat: if it had not been for this patient, long-suffering, never-wearying love of the Spirit of God for me, I would be in hell today.

Now let us consider Ephesians 4:30: *"And do not grieve the Holy Spirit of God, by whom you were sealed for the day of redemption."* Here grief is ascribed to the Holy Spirit. In other words, the Holy Spirit is not a mere blind impersonal influence or power that comes to dwell in your heart and mine. He is a person—a person who loves us, a person who is holy and intensely sensitive toward sin, a person who recoils from sin in what we call its slightest forms as the holiest person on earth never recoiled from sin in its grossest and most repulsive forms.

The Holy Spirit sees whatever we do; He hears whatever we say; He knows our very thoughts. Not a wandering thought is allowed a moment's lodging in our minds without His knowing it. If there is anything impure, unholy, immodest, untrue, harsh, or unChristlike in any way, He is grieved beyond expression. This truth about the Holy Spirit is a wonderful thought. It is the strongest incentive of which I know to walk a Christian walk.

How many a young man is kept back from doing things that he would otherwise do by the thought that, if he did do them, his mother might hear about his actions and be grieved beyond expression? Many a young man has come to the big city and, in some hour of temptation, has been about to go into a place that no self-respecting man ought ever to enter. But just as his hand has been on the doorknob and he has been about to open the door, the thought has come to him, "If I go in, Mother might hear about it. If she did, it would nearly kill her," and he has turned away without entering.

There is One holier than the holiest mother that any of us has ever known, One who loves us with a tenderer love than the love with which our own mothers love us, One who sees everything we do, not only in the daylight but under the cover of night. He hears every word we utter, every careless word that escapes our lips. He knows our every thought; yes, He knows every fleeting notion that we allow a moment's entertainment in our minds. If there is anything unholy, impure, immodest, improper, unkind, harsh, or unChristlike in any way, in act or word or thought, He sees it and is grieved beyond expression.

Oh, how often there has come into my mind some thought or imagination—I do not know from what source—that I ought not to entertain. Just as I have been about to dwell on it, the thought has come, "The Holy Spirit sees that and will be grieved by it," and the improper thought has left.

Keeping this truth about the Holy Spirit in our minds will help us to solve all the questions that perplex the young believer today. Take, for example, the question, "Should I as a Christian go to the movies?" Well, if you go, the Holy Spirit will go, for He dwells in the heart of every believer and goes wherever the believer goes. Would the atmosphere of the place be congenial to the Holy Spirit? If not, do not go. "Should I as a Christian go to a dance?" Well, here again, if you go, the Holy Spirit will surely go. Would the atmosphere of the place be congenial to the Holy Spirit? If not, do not go. "Should I as a Christian go somewhere with my friends to play cards?" Would the atmosphere of the place be congenial to the Holy Spirit? If not, do not go. With the questions that come up and that some of us find so hard to settle, this thought of the Holy Spirit will help you to settle them all, and to settle them right—if you really desire to settle them right and not merely to do the thing that pleases you.

Characteristics Revealed in the Old Testament

Now let us look at a passage in the Old Testament:

> *You also gave Your good Spirit to instruct them, and did not withhold Your manna from their mouth, and gave them water for their thirst.* (Neh. 9:20)

In this verse, both intelligence and goodness are ascribed to the Holy Spirit. This passage does not add anything to what I have already said on this matter; I include it simply because it is from the Old Testament. There are those who say that the doctrine of the personhood of the Holy Spirit is in the New Testament but is not in the Old Testament. But here we find it as clearly in the Old Testament as in the New. Of course, we do not find it as frequently in the Old Testament, for the dispensation of the Holy Spirit began in the New Testament. But the doctrine of the personhood of the Holy Spirit is most certainly in the Old Testament.

The Holy Spirit Performs Actions That Only a Person Could Perform

The second proof of the personhood of the Holy Spirit is this: many actions are ascribed to the Holy Spirit that only a person could perform. Many biblical examples illustrate this point, but I will limit our consideration to three instances.

The Holy Spirit Searches the Deep Things of God

We will first consider 1 Corinthians 2:10: *"But God has revealed them to us through His Spirit. For the Spirit searches all things, yes, the deep things of God."* Here the Holy Spirit is represented as searching the deep things of God. In other words, as I have already said, the Holy Spirit is not a mere illumination whereby our minds are made clear and strong to comprehend truth that we would not otherwise discover. The Holy Spirit is a person who searches the deep things of God and reveals to us the things that He discovers. Such words could only be spoken of a person.

The Holy Spirit Prays

In Romans 8:26, we read,

Likewise the Spirit also helps in our weaknesses. For we do not know what we should pray for as we ought, but the Spirit Himself makes intercession for us with groanings which cannot be uttered.

Here the Holy Spirit is represented as doing what only a person could do—praying. The Holy Spirit is not a mere influence that comes to impel us to prayer. He is not a mere guidance to us in offering our prayers. He is a person who Himself prays. Every believer in Christ has two divine Persons praying for him. First, the Son, our Advocate with the Father, who always lives to make intercession for us at the right hand of God in the place of power (1 John 2:1; Heb. 7:25). Second, the Holy Spirit, who prays through us on earth. Oh, what a wonderful thought, that we have these two divine Persons praying for us every day! What a sense it gives us of our security.

The Holy Spirit Teaches

Now let us consider two other closely related passages. First, John 14:26:

> *But the Helper, the Holy Spirit, whom the Father will send in My name, He will teach you all things, and bring to your remembrance all things that I said to you.*

Here the Holy Spirit is represented as doing what only a person could do, namely, teaching. We have the same thought in John 16:12–14:

> *I still have many things to say to you, but you cannot bear them now. However, when He, the Spirit of truth, has come, He will guide you into all truth; for He will not speak on His own authority, but whatever He hears He will speak; and He will tell you things to come. He will glorify Me, for He will take of what is Mine and declare it to you.*

Here, again, the Holy Spirit is represented as a living, personal teacher. It is our privilege to have the living person of the Holy Spirit today as our Teacher. Every time we study our Bibles, it is possible for us to have this divine Person, the author of the Book, interpret it for us and teach us its meaning.

This truth about the Holy Spirit is a precious thought. When we have heard some great human teacher whom God has made a special blessing to us, many of us have thought, "Oh, if I could only hear that person every day, then I might make some progress in my Christian life." But every day we can have a teacher far more competent than the greatest human teacher who has ever spoken—the Holy Spirit.

The Holy Spirit Is Treated in Ways That Only a Person Could Be Treated

There is another proof of the personhood of the Holy Spirit: the Bible describes the Holy Spirit as being treated in ways that only a person could be treated. In Isaiah 63:10, we are taught that the Holy Spirit is *"rebelled* [against]" and *"grieved."* You cannot rebel against or grieve a mere influence or power. Only a person can be rebelled against and grieved. In Hebrews 10:29, we are taught that the Holy Spirit is *"insulted."* One cannot insult an influence or power, only a person. In Acts 5:3, we are taught that people can *"lie to the Holy Spirit."* One can only lie to a person. In Matthew 12:31, we are taught that the Holy Spirit is *"blaspheme*[d] *against."* We are told that blasphemy against the Holy Spirit is more serious than blasphemy against the Lord Jesus (v. 32), and this certainly could only be said of a person, and a divine person.

The Holy Spirit Fills an Office That Only a Person Could Fill

The fourth proof of the personhood of the Holy Spirit is that an office is attributed to the Holy Spirit that could only be attributed to a person. Look, for example, at John 14:16–17. Here we read,

> And I will pray the Father, and He will give you another Helper, that He may abide with you forever; the Spirit of truth, whom the world cannot receive, because it neither sees

*Him nor knows Him; but you know Him, for
He dwells with you and will be in you.*

Here the Holy Spirit is represented as *"another
Helper"* who was coming to take the place of our
Lord Jesus. Up to this time, our Lord Jesus had always been the Friend at hand to help the disciples in
every emergency that arose. But now He was leaving, and their hearts were filled with consternation.
He told them that although He was going, Another
was coming to take His place. Can you imagine our
Lord Jesus saying this if the One who was coming to
take His place had been a mere impersonal influence
or power? If the One who was coming to take His
place had not been another person but a mere influence or power, I could not imagine our Lord Jesus
saying what He said in John 16:7,

*Nevertheless I tell you the truth. It is to your
advantage that I go away; for if I do not go
away, the Helper will not come to you; but if I
depart, I will send Him to you.*

Is it conceivable for one moment for our Lord to
say that it was to their advantage for Him, a divine
person, to leave and for a mere influence or power,
no matter how divine, to come to take His place? No!
What our Lord said was that He, one divine Person,
was going, but that another Person, just as divine,
was coming to take His place.

To me, this promise is one of the most precious
promises in the whole Word of God. During the ab-
sence of my Lord, until that glad day when He will

come back again, another Person, just as divine as He, is by my side—yes, dwells in my heart every moment to commune with me and to help me in every emergency that can possibly arise.

The Meaning of the Word "Helper"

I suppose you know that the Greek word translated *"Helper"* in these verses means helper plus a whole lot besides. The Greek word so translated is *parakletos.* This word is a compound word, made up of the word *para,* which means "alongside," and *kletos,* which means "one called." So *parakletos* means "one called to stand alongside another"—to take his part and help him in every emergency that arises.

Parakletos is the word that is translated *"Advocate"* in 1 John 2:1: *"If anyone sins, we have an Advocate with the Father, Jesus Christ the righteous."* But the word *"Advocate"* does not give the full force of the word *parakletos.* Etymologically, it means about the same. *Advocate* is a Latin word transliterated into the English. The word is a compound word made up of *ad,* meaning "to," and *vocatus,* meaning "one called," that is to say, "one called to another to take his part, to help him." But in our English usage, the word *advocate* has obtained a restricted sense. The Greek word, as I have already said, means "one called alongside another," and the thought is of a helper always at hand with his counsel and his strength and any form of help needed.

Up to this time, the Lord Jesus Himself had been the disciples' Paraclete, or their Friend always at hand to help. Whenever they got into any trouble, they simply turned to Jesus. For example, on one occasion they were perplexed about the subject of prayer. They said to Him, *"Lord, teach us to pray"* (Luke 11:1), and He taught them to pray. On another occasion, Jesus was coming to them by walking on the water. When their first fear was over and He had said, *"It is I; do not be afraid"* (Matt. 14:27), Peter said to Him, *"Lord, if it is You, command me to come to You on the water"* (v. 28). The Lord said to him, *"Come"* (v. 29). Then Peter clambered over the side of the fishing boat and started to go to Jesus by walking on the water. Seemingly, he turned around, took his eyes off the Lord, and looked at the fishing boat to see if the other disciples were noticing how well he was doing. But no sooner had he taken his eyes off the Lord and focused on his fears than he began to sink. He cried out, *"Lord, save me!"* (v. 30), and Jesus reached out His hand and held him up.

In the same way, when the disciples got into any other emergency, they turned to the Lord, and He delivered them. Now He was leaving, and, as I said, consternation filled their hearts. But the Lord said to them, "Yes, I am going, but Another just as divine, just as able to help, is coming to take my place." This other Paraclete is with us wherever we go, every hour of the day or night. He is always by our side.

The Cure for Fear

If this thought gets into your heart and stays there, you will never have another moment of fear no matter how long you live. How can we fear in any circumstance if He is by our side? You may be surrounded by a howling mob, but what of it if He walks between you and the mob? This thought will banish all fear.

I had a striking illustration of this truth in my own experience some years ago. I was speaking at a Bible conference at Lake Kenka in New York State. A cousin of mine had a cottage four miles up the lake, and I went there and spent my day off with him. The next day he brought me down in his boat to where the conference was being held. As I stepped off the boat onto the pier, he said to me, "Come back again tonight and spend the night with us," and I promised him that I would. But I did not realize what I was promising.

That night, after the meeting, as I left the hotel and started on my walk, I found that I had undertaken a very difficult task. The cottage was four miles away, and a four-mile walk or an eight-mile walk was nothing under ordinary circumstances. But a storm was brewing; the whole sky was overcast. The path led along a cliff bordering the lake, and the path was near the edge of the cliff. Sometimes the lake was perhaps not more than ten or twelve feet below; at other times it was some thirty or forty feet below. I had never traveled on the path before, and since there was no starlight, I could not see the path at all. Furthermore, there had already been a storm that had torn out deep ditches across the path into which one might fall and break his leg. I could not see these ditches except when there was a sudden flash of lightning. I would see one, and then my surroundings would be darker and I would be blinder than ever.

As I walked along this path with all its furrows, so near the edge of the cliff, I felt it was perilous to make the trip and thought of going back. Then the thought came to me, "You promised that you would come tonight, and they might be sitting up waiting for you." So I felt that I must go on. But it seemed creepy and uncanny to walk along the edge of that cliff on a path that I could not see. I could only hear the sobbing and wailing and moaning of the lake at the foot of the cliff. Then the thought came to me, "What was it that you told the people there at the conference about the Holy Spirit being a person always by our side?" At once I realized that the Holy Spirit walked between me and the edge of the cliff, and that four miles through the dark was four miles without a fear—a cheerful instead of a fearful walk.

I once explained this thought in the Royal Albert Hall in London one dark, dismal February afternoon. There was a young lady in the audience who was very much afraid of the dark. It simply seemed impossible for her to go into a dark room alone. After the meeting was over, she hurried home and rushed into the room where her mother was sitting and cried, "Oh, Mother, I have heard the most wonderful message this afternoon about the Holy Spirit always being by our side as our ever present Helper and Protector. I will never be afraid of the dark again." Her mother was a practical Englishwoman and said to her, "Well, let us see how real this is. Go upstairs to the top floor, into the dark room; shut the door, and stay in there alone in the dark." The daughter went bounding up the stairs, went into the dark room, and closed the door. It was pitch dark. "Oh," she wrote me the next day, "it was dark, utterly dark, but that room was bright and glorious with the presence of the Holy Spirit."

The Cure for Insomnia

In this thought is also the cure for insomnia. Have you ever had insomnia? I have. For two dark, awful years. Night after night, I would go to bed, almost dead, as it seemed to me, for lack of sleep, and I thought I would certainly sleep since I could hardly stay awake. But scarcely had my head touched the pillow when I knew I would not sleep. I would hear the clock strike twelve, one, two, three, four, five, six, and then it was time to get up. It seemed as though I did not sleep at all, though I have no doubt I did, for I believe that people who suffer from insomnia sleep more than they think they do, or else they would die. But it seemed as if I did not sleep at all, and this went on for two whole years, until I thought that if I could not get sleep I would lose my mind.

Then I received deliverance. For years after being delivered, I would retire and fall asleep about as soon as my head touched the pillow. But one night I went to bed in the Bible Institute in Chicago, where I was then staying. I expected to fall asleep almost immediately, as had become my custom, but scarcely had my head touched the pillow when I knew I was not going to sleep. Insomnia was back. If you have ever had it, you will always recognize it. It seemed as if Insomnia were sitting on the foot of my bed looking like an imp, grinning at me and saying, "I'm back for two more years."

"Oh," I thought, "two more years of this awful insomnia." But that very morning I had been teaching the students in the lecture room on the floor below about the personhood of the Holy Spirit, and the thought came to me almost immediately, "What was that you were telling the students downstairs this morning about the Holy Spirit always being with us?" And I said, "Why don't you practice what you preach?" I looked up and said, "O blessed Holy Spirit of God, You are here. If You have anything to say to me, I will listen." And He opened to me some of the sweet and precious things about Jesus Christ, filling my soul with calm and peace and joy. The next thing I knew I was asleep, and then it was the next morning. Whenever Insomnia has come around since and sat on the foot of my bed, I have done the same thing, and relying on the Holy Spirit has never failed.

The Cure for Loneliness

Also in this thought of the Holy Spirit as our Helper is a cure for all loneliness. If the thought of the Holy Spirit as an ever present friend once enters your heart and stays there, you will never have another lonely moment as long as you live. For the majority of the last sixteen years, my life has been a lonely life. I have often been separated from my whole family for months at a time. Sometimes I have not seen my wife for two or three months, and for eighteen months I was with my wife but did not see any other member of my family.

One night I was walking the deck of a ship in the South Seas between New Zealand and Tasmania.

It was a stormy night. Most of the other passengers were below, sick; none of the officers or sailors could walk with me because they had their hands full looking after the boat. I walked the deck alone. Four of the five other members of my family were on the other side of the globe, seventeen thousand miles away by the nearest route that I could get to them. And the one member of my family who was nearer was not with me that night. As I walked the deck alone, I got to thinking about my four children seventeen thousand miles away and was about to get lonesome when the thought came to me of the Holy Spirit by my side. I knew that as I walked He took every step with me, and all loneliness was gone.

I expressed this thought some years ago in the city of Saint Paul. At the close of the meeting, a physician came to me and said, "I wish to thank you for that thought. I am often called to go out alone at night, through darkness and storm, to attend to a sick patient, and I have been very lonely. But I will never be lonely again, for I will know that every mile of the way the Holy Spirit is beside me."

The Cure for a Broken Heart

In this same precious truth there is a cure for a broken heart. Oh, how many brokenhearted people there are in the world today! Many of us have lost loved ones. But we need not have a moment's heartache if we only know *"the communion of the Holy Spirit"* (2 Cor. 13:14). There is perhaps some woman who a year ago, or a few months ago, or a few weeks ago, or a few days ago, had by her side a man whom she dearly loved, a man so strong and wise that she was freed from all sense of responsibility and care, for all the burdens were on him. How bright and happy life was in his companionship. But the dark day came when that loved one was taken away, and how lonely, empty, barren, and full of burden and care life is today! Listen! There is One who walks right by your side, wiser and stronger and more loving than the wisest and strongest and most loving husband who has ever lived, ready to bear all the burdens and responsibilities of life. Yes, He is ready to do far more. He is ready to come and dwell in your heart and fill every nook and corner of your empty, aching heart, and thus banish all loneliness and heartache forever.

I made this statement one afternoon in Saint Andrews Hall in Glasgow. At the close of the meeting, when I went to the reception room, a lady who had hurried along to meet me approached me. She wore the customary clothing of a widow, her face bore the marks of deep sorrow, but now there was a happy look in her face. She hurried to me and said, "Doctor Torrey, this is the anniversary of my dear husband's death," (her husband was one of the most highly esteemed Christian men in Glasgow) "and I came to Saint Andrews Hall today saying to myself, 'Doctor Torrey will have something to say that will help me.' Oh," she continued, "you have said just the right thing! I will never be lonesome again, never have a heartache again. I will let the Holy Spirit come in and fill every aching corner of my heart."

Eighteen months passed. I was in Scotland again, taking a short vacation on the Clyde River on the private yacht of a friend. One day, when we stopped, a little boat came alongside the yacht. The first one who clambered up the side of the yacht and onto the deck was this widow. Seeing me standing on the deck, she hurried across and took my hand in both of hers, and with a radiant smile on her face she said, "Oh, Doctor Torrey, the thought you gave me in Saint Andrews Hall that afternoon stays with me still, and I have not had a lonely or sad hour from that day to this."

Help in Our Christian Work

It is in our Christian work that this thought comes to us with the greatest power and helpfulness. Take my own experience as an example. I became a minister simply because I had to or be forever lost. I do not mean that I am saved by preaching the Gospel. I am saved simply on the ground of Christ's atoning blood and that alone, but my becoming a Christian and accepting Him as my Savior depended on my preaching the Gospel. For six years I refused to become a Christian because I was unwilling to preach, and I felt that if I became a Christian I must preach. The night that I was converted I did not say, "I will accept Christ" or "I will give up my sins." I said, "I will preach."

But if there was ever a man who by natural temperament was unfit to preach, it was I. I was an abnormally bashful boy. A stranger could scarcely speak to me without my blushing to the roots of my hair. Of all the tortures I endured at school, none was so great as that of reciting in front of the class.

To stand up on the platform and have all the other students looking at me—I could scarcely endure it. When I had to recite and my own mother and father asked me to recite to them before I went to school, I simply could not recite in front of my own parents. Think of a man like that going into the ministry!

Even after I started attending Yale College, when I would go home on a vacation and my mother would have visitors and send for me to come in and meet them, I could not say a word. After they were gone, my mother would say to me, "Archie, why didn't you say something to Mrs. So-and-So," and I would say, "Why, Mother, I did!" She would reply, "You didn't utter a sound." I thought I had, but the sound would come no farther than my throat and would there be smothered.

I was so bashful that I would never even speak in a church prayer meeting until after I entered the theological seminary. Then I thought that if I was to be a preacher, I must at least be able to speak in my own church prayer meeting. Making up my mind that I would, I learned a little message by heart. I remember some of it now, but I think I forgot much of it when I got up to speak that night. As soon as the meeting started, I grasped the back of the seat in front of me, pulled myself up to my feet, and held on to that seat so that I would not fall. I tremblingly repeated as much of my little message as I could remember and then dropped back into my seat. At the close of the meeting, a dear old lady, a lovely Christian woman, came to me and encouragingly said, "Oh, Mr. Torrey, I want to thank you for what you said tonight. It did me so much good. You spoke with so much feeling." Feeling! The only feeling I had was that I was scared nearly to death. Think of a man like that going into the ministry!

My first years in the ministry were torture. I would preach three times each Sunday. I would commit my sermons to memory, and then I would stand up and twist the top button of my coat until I had twisted the sermon out. Then, when the third sermon was preached and finished, I would drop back into my seat with a great sense of relief that that was over for another week. Then the thought would take hold of me, "Well, you have to begin tomorrow morning to get ready for next Sunday!"

But a glad day came when the truth I am trying to teach you took possession of me. That truth is this: when I stood up to preach, though people saw me, there was Another who stood by my side whom they did not see, but upon whom was all the responsibility for the meeting. All that I had to do was to get as far back out of sight as possible and let Him do the preaching. From that day, preaching has been the joy of my life. I would rather preach than eat. Sometimes, when I rise to preach, before I have uttered a word, the thought of Him standing beside me, able and willing to take charge of the whole meeting and do whatever needs to be done, has so filled my heart with exultant joy that I have felt like shouting.

The same thought applies to Sunday school teaching. Perhaps you worry about your Sunday school class for fear that you will say something that ought not to be said, or leave unsaid something that ought to be said. The thought of the burden and responsibility almost crushes you. Listen! Always remember this as you teach your class: there is One right beside you who knows just what ought to be said and just what ought to be done. Instead of carrying the responsibility of the class, let Him carry it; let Him do the teaching.

One Monday morning I met one of the most faithful laymen I have ever known, and a very gifted Bible teacher. He was deep in the blues over his failure with his class the day before—at least, what he regarded as failure. He unburdened his heart to me. I said to him, "Mr. Dyer, did you not ask God to give you wisdom as you went before that class?" He said, "I did." I said, "Did you not expect Him to give it?" He said, "I did." Then I said, "What right have you to doubt that He did?" He replied, "I never thought of that before. I will never worry about my class again."

The same thought applies to personal ministry. At the close of a meeting, when the pastor urges those who are saved to go and speak to someone about his soul's salvation, oh, how many of you want to go, but you do not stir. You think to yourself, "I might say the wrong thing." You will if *you* say it. You will certainly say the wrong thing. But trust the Holy Spirit—He will say the right thing. Let Him have your lips to speak through. It may not appear the right thing at the time, but sometime you will find out that it was just the right thing.

One night in Launceston, Tasmania, as Mrs. Torrey and I left the meeting, my wife said to me, "Archie, I wasted my whole evening. I have been talking to the most frivolous girl. I don't think that she has a serious thought in her head." I replied, "Clara, how do you know? Did you not trust God to guide you?" "Yes." "Well, leave it with Him." The very next night at the close of the meeting, the same seemingly frivolous girl came up to Mrs. Torrey, leading her mother by the hand, and said, "Mrs. Torrey, won't you speak to my mother? You led me to Christ last night; now please lead my mother to Christ."

CONCLUSION

So we see by these many examples that the Holy Spirit is a person. Theoretically, you probably believed this before, but do you, in your real thoughts of Him, in your practical attitude toward Him, treat Him as a person? Do you really regard Him as just as real a person as Jesus Christ is—as loving, as wise, as strong, as worthy of our confidence and love and surrender? Do you see Him as a divine person always by your side?

After our Lord's departure, the Holy Spirit came into this world to be to the disciples, and to be to us, what Jesus Christ had been to them during the days of His personal companionship with them. Is He that to you today? Do you know *"the communion of the Holy Spirit"* (2 Cor. 13:14)—the companionship of the Holy Spirit, the partnership of the Holy Spirit, the fellowship of the Holy Spirit, the comradeship of the Holy Spirit? To put it simply, the whole purpose of this chapter—I say it reverently—is to introduce you to my Friend, the Holy Spirit.

Is the Holy Spirit God, and Is He Separate from the Father and Son?

7

Is the Holy Spirit God, and Is He Separate from the Father and Son?

The grace of the Lord Jesus Christ, and the love
of God, and the communion of the
Holy Spirit be with you all.
—2 Corinthians 13:14

In the previous chapter, I wrote about the personhood of the Holy Spirit. We saw clearly that the Holy Spirit is a person. I referred to His deity in passing but did not dwell on it; so the question remains, Is the Holy Spirit a divine person? And still another question remains: If the Holy Spirit is a divine person, is He separate and distinct from the Father and the Son? In this chapter, we will consider what the Bible teaches on these subjects.

PROOFS OF THE DEITY OF THE HOLY SPIRIT

First, let us examine the question of the deity of the Holy Spirit. The fact that the Holy Spirit is a person does not prove that He is divine. There are spirits who are persons but are not God. However, there are five distinct proofs of the deity of the Holy Spirit.

The Holy Spirit's Divine Attributes Prove His Deity

The first proof that the Holy Spirit is God is that four distinctively divine attributes are ascribed to the Holy Spirit in the Bible. As I mentioned in the chapter on the deity of Christ, when I speak of distinctively divine attributes, I am speaking of attributes that God alone possesses. Any person who has these attributes must therefore be God. These four distinctively divine attributes are omnipotence, omniscience, omnipresence, and eternity.

Omnipotence

First of all, omnipotence is ascribed to the Holy Spirit. Take, for example, Luke 1:35:

> *And the angel answered and said to her, "The Holy Spirit will come upon you, and the power of the Highest will overshadow you; therefore, also, that Holy One who is to be born will be called the Son of God."*

This passage plainly declares that the Holy Spirit has the power of the Highest, that He is omnipotent.

Omniscience

In the second place, omniscience is ascribed to the Holy Spirit. This is done, for example, in 1 Corinthians 2:10–11:

> *But God has revealed them to us through His Spirit. For the Spirit searches all things, yes,*

*the deep things of God. For what man knows
the things of a man except the spirit of the man
which is in him? Even so no one knows the
things of God except the Spirit of God.*

Here we are distinctly told that the Holy Spirit
searches all things and knows all things, even the
deep things of God.

We find the same thought again in John 14:26:

*But the Helper, the Holy Spirit, whom the Fa-
ther will send in My name, He will teach you
all things, and bring to your remembrance all
things that I said to you.*

Here we are distinctly told that the Holy Spirit
teaches all things; therefore, He must know all
things.

This truth is stated even more explicitly in John
16:12–13:

*I still have many things to say to you, but you
cannot bear them now. However, when He, the
Spirit of truth, has come, He will guide you
into all truth; for He will not speak on His
own authority, but whatever He hears He will
speak; and He will tell you things to come.*

In all these passages, it is either directly declared or unmistakably implied that the Holy Spirit
knows all things, that He is omniscient.

Omnipresence

In the third place, omnipresence is ascribed to
the Holy Spirit. We find this in Psalm 139:7–10:

> *Where can I go from Your Spirit? Or where*
> *can I flee from Your presence? If I ascend into*
> *heaven, You are there; if I make my bed in*
> *hell, behold, You are there. If I take the wings*
> *of the morning, and dwell in the uttermost*
> *parts of the sea, even there Your hand shall*
> *lead me, and Your right hand shall hold me.*

Here we are told in the most explicit and unmistakable way that the Spirit of God, the Holy Spirit, is everywhere. There is no place in heaven, earth, or hades where we can go from His presence.

Eternity

Eternity is also ascribed to the Holy Spirit. This we find in Hebrews 9:14, where we read,

> *How much more shall the blood of Christ, who*
> *through the eternal Spirit offered Himself*
> *without spot to God, cleanse your conscience*
> *from dead works to serve the living God?*

Here we find the words *"the eternal Spirit"* just as elsewhere we find the words *"the eternal God"* (Deut. 33:27).

Putting these different passages together, we see clearly that each of four distinctively divine attributes, four attributes that no one but God possesses, is ascribed to the Holy Spirit.

The Holy Spirit's Divine Works Prove His Deity

The second proof of the true deity of the Holy Spirit is found in the fact that three distinctively divine works are ascribed to the Holy Spirit. That is to say, the Holy Spirit is said to do three things that God alone can do.

Creation

The first of these distinctively divine works is the one that we always think of first when we think of God's work—the work of creation. We find creation ascribed to the Holy Spirit in Job 33:4: *"The Spirit of God has made me, and the breath of the Almighty gives me life."* We find the same thing implied in Psalm 104:30: *"You send forth Your Spirit, they are created; and You renew the face of the earth."* In these two passages, the most distinctively divine of all works—the work of creation—is ascribed to the Holy Spirit.

Impartation of Life

The impartation of life is also ascribed to the Holy Spirit. This we find, for example, in John 6:63: *"It is the Spirit who gives life; the flesh profits nothing."* We find the same thing again in Romans 8:11:

> *But if the Spirit of Him who raised Jesus from the dead dwells in you, He who raised Christ from the dead will also give life to your mortal bodies through His Spirit who dwells in you.*

In this passage, we do not have merely the impartation of life to the spirit of man, but the impartation of life to the body of man in the resurrection.

Man's creation and the impartation of life to man are ascribed to the operation of the Holy Spirit in the first book in the Bible, where we read,

> And the LORD God formed man of the dust of the ground, and breathed into his nostrils the breath of life; and man became a living being.
> *(Gen. 2:7)*

Here we are told that man was created and became a living soul through God's breathing into him the breath of life. These words clearly imply that man's creation was through the instrumentality of the Holy Spirit, for the Holy Spirit is the breath of God going out in a personal way.

Authorship of Divine Prophecies

The third divine work ascribed to the Holy Spirit is the authorship of divine prophecies. We find this, for example, in 2 Peter 1:21: *"For prophecy never came by the will of man, but holy men of God spoke as they were moved by the Holy Spirit."* Here we are distinctly told that it was through the operation of the Holy Spirit that men were made the mouthpiece of God and uttered God's truth. We find this same thought in the Old Testament in 2 Samuel 23:2–3: *"The Spirit of the LORD spoke by me, and His word was on my tongue. The God of Israel said, the Rock of Israel spoke to me."* In this passage, the authorship of God's prophecies is ascribed to the Holy Spirit.

Putting all these passages together, we see that three distinctively divine works are ascribed to the Holy Spirit.

A Comparison of Old Testament and New Testament Verses Proves His Deity

The third proof of the deity of the Holy Spirit is found in the fact that passages that refer to Jehovah in the Old Testament are taken to refer to the Holy Spirit in the New Testament. There are numerous instances of this—not as numerous as in the case of Jesus Christ the Son, yet enough to make it perfectly clear that the Holy Spirit occupies the same place in New Testament thought that Jehovah occupies in Old Testament thought.

Isaiah 6:8–10 and Acts 28:25–27

A striking illustration of this is found in Isaiah 6:8–10, where we read,

Also I heard the voice of the Lord, saying: "Whom shall I send, and who will go for Us?" Then I said, "Here am I! Send me." And He said, "Go, and tell this people: 'Keep on hearing, but do not understand; keep on seeing, but do not perceive.' Make the heart of this people dull, and their ears heavy, and shut their eyes; lest they see with their eyes, and hear with their ears, and understand with their heart, and return and be healed."

Here we are distinctly told it is *"the Lord"*—and the context shows that *"the Lord"* is the Lord Jehovah—who is speaking. But when we turn to Acts 28:25–27, we read these words:

> *So when they did not agree among themselves, they departed after Paul had said one word: "The Holy Spirit spoke rightly through Isaiah the prophet to our fathers* [notice that in the passage in Isaiah we are told it is the Lord Jehovah who spoke, and here we are told by Paul that it is the Holy Spirit who spoke through the prophet], *saying, 'Go to this people and say: "Hearing you will hear, and shall not understand; and seeing you will see, and not perceive; for the hearts of this people have grown dull. Their ears are hard of hearing, and their eyes they have closed, lest they should see with their eyes and hear with their ears, lest they should understand with their hearts and turn, so that I should heal them.""'*

In the Old Testament, we are told that the Lord Jehovah is the speaker; in the New Testament, we read that the Holy Spirit is the speaker. The Holy Spirit occupies the place in New Testament thought that the Lord Jehovah occupies in Old Testament thought.

It is notable that this same passage is applied to Jesus Christ in John 12:39–41. In the same chapter of Isaiah, in the threefold *"holy"* (Isa. 6:3) in the seraphic cry, do we not have a hint of the tripersonhood of Jehovah of Hosts? Is it then not proper to have a threefold application of Isaiah's vision?

Exodus 16:7 and Hebrews 3:7–9

Another illustration of a statement that in the Old Testament refers to Jehovah but in the New Testament refers to the Holy Spirit, is found by a comparison of Exodus 16:7 with Hebrews 3:7–9. In Exodus 16:7, we read,

> *And in the morning you shall see the glory of the LORD; for He hears your complaints against the LORD. But what are we, that you complain against us?*

Here we are told that the murmuring and provocation of the children of Israel in the wilderness were against Jehovah. But in Hebrews 3:7–9, we read,

> *Therefore, as the Holy Spirit says: "Today, if you will hear His voice, do not harden your hearts as in the rebellion, in the day of trial in the wilderness, where your fathers tested Me, tried Me, and saw My works forty years."*

In this New Testament passage, we are told that it was the Holy Spirit whom they provoked in the wilderness. It is clear that the Holy Spirit occupies here in New Testament thought the position Jehovah occupies in Exodus 16:7 in Old Testament thought.

To sum up the passages in this section, we see that statements that in the Old Testament distinctly name the Lord, God, or Jehovah as their subject are applied to the Holy Spirit in the New Testament. That is to say, the Holy Spirit occupies the position of Deity in New Testament thought.

The Name of the Holy Spirit Coupled with That of the Father and of the Son Proves His Deity

The fourth way that the deity of the Holy Spirit is clearly taught in the New Testament is that the name of the Holy Spirit is coupled with that of the Father and of the Son in a way in which it would be impossible for a reverent and thoughtful mind to couple the name of any finite being with that of Deity. There are numerous illustrations of this point. Three will suffice for our present purpose.

We read, for example, in 1 Corinthians 12:4–6:

> *There are diversities of gifts, but the same Spirit. There are differences of ministries, but the same Lord. And there are diversities of activities, but it is the same God who works all in all.*

In this passage, we see the name of the Holy Spirit coupled with that of God and of the Lord on a ground of equality.

We see the same thing again in Matthew 28:19: *"Go therefore and make disciples of all the nations, baptizing them in the name of the Father and of the Son and of the Holy Spirit."* If the Holy Spirit were not God, it would be shocking to couple His name in this way with that of God the Father and of the Lord Jesus His Son.

Another striking illustration is found in 2 Corinthians 13:14: *"The grace of the Lord Jesus Christ, and the love of God, and the communion of the Holy Spirit be with you all."* Here the name of the Holy Spirit is coupled on a ground of equality with that of the Father and of the Son.

In all these passages, as we have seen, the name of the Holy Spirit is coupled with that of God in a way in which it would be impossible for an intelligent worshiper of the Lord to couple the name of any finite being with that of Deity.

The Fact That the Holy Spirit Is Called God Proves His Deity

The fifth way, and perhaps the most decisive way, in which the deity of the Holy Spirit is taught in the Bible, is that the Holy Spirit in so many words is called God. This we find in Acts 5:3–4:

> But Peter said, "Ananias, why has Satan filled your heart to lie to the Holy Spirit and keep back part of the price of the land for yourself? While it remained, was it not your own? And after it was sold, was it not in your own control? Why have you conceived this thing in your heart? You have not lied to men but to God."

In the third verse, we are distinctly told that it was the Holy Spirit to whom Ananias had lied, while in the fourth verse, we are told that it was God to whom Ananias had lied. Putting the two statements together, we clearly see that the Holy Spirit is God.

All These Facts about the Holy Spirit Combined Prove His Deity

Allow me to sum up all that I have said about the deity of the Holy Spirit. We see that the Holy Spirit is a divine person by the following: several distinctively divine attributes are ascribed to the Holy Spirit; several distinctively divine works are ascribed to the Holy Spirit; statements that in the Old Testament distinctly name Jehovah, the Lord, or God as their subject distinctly name the Holy Spirit in the New Testament; the name of the Holy Spirit is coupled with that of God in a way in which it would be impossible to couple the name of any finite being with that of Deity; the Holy Spirit is called God.

In all these unmistakable ways, God distinctly proclaims in His Word that the Holy Spirit is a divine person. It is absolutely impossible for anyone who goes to the Bible to find out what it actually teaches—and not merely to twist and distort it to fit into his own preconceived notions—to come to any other conclusion than that the Holy Spirit is God.

PROOFS OF THE DISTINCTION BETWEEN THE FATHER, THE SON, AND THE HOLY SPIRIT

But now we come to the question, Is the Holy Spirit a person who is distinct from the Father and from the Son? He might be a person, as we have clearly seen that He is, and He might be a divine person, as we have just seen that He is. But at the same time, He might be only the same person who manifested Himself at times as the Father and at other times as the Son. In this case, there would not be three divine Persons in the Godhead, but one divine Person who variously manifested Himself as Father, Son, and Holy Spirit. So, again, the question that confronts us is, Is the Holy Spirit a person who is separate and distinct from the Father and from the Son? This question is plainly answered in various passages in the New Testament.

Verses That Prove the Distinctiveness of the Person of the Holy Spirit

In the first place, we find this question answered in John 14:26 and John 15:26. In John 14:26, we read,

> *But the Helper, the Holy Spirit, whom the Father will send in My name, He will teach you all things, and bring to your remembrance all things that I said to you.*

In John 15:26, we read,

> *But when the Helper comes, whom I shall send to you from the Father, the Spirit of truth who proceeds from the Father, He will testify of Me.*

In both of these passages, we are told that the Holy Spirit is a person entirely distinct from the Father and the Son, that He is sent from the Father by the Son. Elsewhere we are taught that Jesus Christ was sent by the Father. (See John 6:29; 8:29, 42.) In these passages, it is as clear as language can make it that Father, Son, and Holy Spirit are not one and the same Person manifesting Himself in three different forms, but that they are three distinct Persons.

We find clear proof that the Father, Son, and Holy Spirit are three distinct Persons in John 16:13, where we read,

> *However, when He, the Spirit of truth, has come, He will guide you into all truth; for He will not speak on His own authority, but whatever He hears He will speak; and He will tell you things to come.*

In this passage, the clearest possible distinction is drawn between the Holy Spirit who speaks and the One from whom He speaks. We are told in so many words that this One from whom the Spirit speaks is not Himself, but Another.

In the next verse, the same thought is brought out in still another way. In this verse, Jesus said, *"He will glorify Me, for He will take of what is Mine and declare it to you"* (John 16:14). Here the clearest distinction is drawn between *"He,"* the Holy Spirit, and *"Me,"* Jesus Christ. It is the work of the Holy Spirit not to glorify Himself, but Another, and this Other is Jesus Christ. The Holy Spirit takes what belongs to Another—that is, to Christ—and declares it to believers. It would be impossible to express in human language a distinction between two persons more plainly than the distinction between the Son and the Holy Spirit that is expressed in this verse.

The distinction between the Father and the Son and the Holy Spirit is very clearly brought out in Luke 3:21–22:

> *Now it came to pass, when all the people were baptized, that, Jesus also having been baptized, and praying, the heaven was opened, and the Holy Ghost descended in a bodily form, as a dove, upon him, and a voice came out of heaven, Thou art my beloved Son; in thee I am well pleased.* (RV)

Here a clear distinction is drawn between Jesus Christ, who was on the earth; the Father, who spoke to Him from heaven; and the Holy Spirit, who descended from the Father upon the Son in bodily form as a dove.

Still another striking illustration is found in Matthew 28:19: *"Go therefore and make disciples of all the nations, baptizing them in the name of the Father and of the Son and of the Holy Spirit."* Here a clear distinction is drawn between the name of *"the Father"* and the name of *"the Son"* and the name of *"the Holy Spirit."*

A very clear distinction between the Father, Son, and Holy Spirit is found in John 14:16–17: *"And I will pray the Father, and He will give you another Helper, that He may abide with you forever; the Spirit of truth."* Here the clearest possible distinction is drawn between the Son who prays, the Father to whom He prays, and *"another Helper"* who is given in response to the Son's prayer. Nothing could possibly be plainer than the distinction that Jesus Christ made in this passage between Himself and the Father and the Holy Spirit.

We find the same thing again in John 16:7:

> *Nevertheless I tell you the truth. It is to your advantage that I go away; for if I do not go away, the Helper will not come to you; but if I depart, I will send Him to you.*

Here, once more, the Lord Jesus Himself made a clear distinction between Himself, who was about to go away, and the Holy Spirit, the other Helper who was coming to take His place after He had gone away.

The same thing is brought out again in Acts 2:33 in Peter's sermon on the Day of Pentecost, in which Peter is recorded as saying about Jesus,

> *Therefore being exalted to the right hand of God, and having received from the Father the promise of the Holy Spirit, He poured out this which you now see and hear.*

Here a clear distinction is drawn between the Son, who was exalted to the right hand of the Father, the Father Himself, and the Holy Spirit, whom the Son received from the Father and poured out on the church.

The Doctrine of the Trinity

In summary, let me say that again and again the Bible draws the clearest possible distinction between the Holy Spirit, the Father, and the Son. They are three separate Persons who have mutual relationships with one another, who speak of or to one another, and who apply the pronouns of the second and third persons to one another.

We have seen that the Bible makes it plain that the Holy Spirit is a divine person and that He is an entirely separate person from the Father and from the Son. In other words, there are three divine Persons in the Godhead. It has often been said that the doctrine of the Trinity is not taught in the Bible. It is true that the doctrine of the Trinity is not directly taught in the Bible in so many words, but this doctrine is simply the putting together of truths that are distinctly and unmistakably taught in the Bible. The Bible clearly states that there is but one God (Deut. 6:4). But it teaches with equal clearness, as we have seen in this chapter, that there are three divine Persons—the Father, the Son, and the Holy Spirit. The doctrine of the Trinity, therefore, is the putting together of these truths, which are taught with equal plainness.

Many people say that the doctrine of the Trinity is in the New Testament but not in the Old Testament. But it is in the very first chapter of the Bible. In Genesis 1:26, we read, *"Then God said, 'Let Us make man in Our image, according to Our likeness.'"* Here the plurality of the persons in the Godhead comes out clearly. God did not say, "I will" or "Let Me make man in My image." He said, *"Let Us make man in Our image, according to Our likeness."*

Moreover, the three persons of the Trinity are found in the first three verses of the Bible. *"In the beginning God created the heavens and the earth"* (Gen. 1:1). There you have God the Father. *"The earth was without form, and void; and darkness was on the face of the deep. And the Spirit of God was hovering over the face of the waters"* (v. 2). There you have the Holy Spirit. *"Then God said"*—there you have the Word—*"'Let there be light'; and there was light"* (v. 3). Here we have the three persons of the Trinity in the first three verses of the Bible.

In fact, the doctrine of the Trinity is found hundreds of times in the Old Testament. In the Hebrew Bible, it is found every place where you find the word *God* in your English Bible, for the Hebrew word for *God* is a plural noun. Literally translated, it would be "Gods," not "God."

The Unitarians and the Jews reject the deity of Christ. They often refer to Deuteronomy 6:4 as conclusive proof that the deity of Christ cannot be true: *"Hear, O Israel: the LORD our God, the LORD is one!"* But the very doctrine that they are seeking to disprove is found in Deuteronomy 6:4, for the literal translation of the verse is, "Hear, O Israel: Jehovah our Gods is one Jehovah."

Why did the Hebrews, with their intense monotheism, use a plural name for God? This question puzzled the Hebrew grammarians and lexicographers. The best explanation they could find was that the plural for God used in the Bible was the "pluralis majestatis" (*we* in place of *I* in the speech of royalty). This explanation is entirely inadequate, to say nothing of the fact that its validity is very doubtful.

Another explanation is far nearer at hand, and far more adequate and satisfactory: the inspired Hebrew writers used a plural name for God in spite of their intense monotheism because there is a plurality of persons in the one Godhead.

Someone may ask, "How can God be three and one at the same time?" The answer to this question is very simple and easily understandable. He cannot be three and one in the same sense, nor does the Bible teach that He is. In what sense can He be one and three? A perfectly satisfactory answer to this question is clearly impossible from the very nature of the case. In the first place, *"God is Spirit"* (John 4:24), and numbers belong primarily to the physical world. Difficulty always arises when we attempt to conceive of spiritual being in the forms of physical thought. In the second place, a perfectly satisfactory answer is impossible because God is infinite and we are finite. God dwells *"in the light which no man can approach unto"* (1 Tim. 6:16 KJV). Our attempts at a philosophical explanation of the triune nature of God are attempts to put the facts of infinite being into the forms of finite thought, and of necessity such attempts can at the very best be only partially successful.

This much we know, that God is essentially one, and also that there are three Persons in this one Godhead. There is but one God, but this one God makes Himself known to us as three distinct Persons—Father, Son, and Holy Spirit. There is one God, eternally existing, and manifesting Himself in three Persons.

If we were to go into the realm of philosophy, it could be shown from the very necessities of the case that, if God was to be God, He had to exist as more than one person. Before the creation of finite beings, there had to be a multiplicity of persons in the eternal Godhead. Otherwise, God could not love, for there would be no one to love, and therefore, God could not be God.

The ease with which one can grasp the Unitarian concept of God is not in its favor but against it.* Any God who could be thoroughly comprehended by a finite mind would not be an infinite God. It would be impossible for a thoroughly intelligent mind to really worship a God whom he could thoroughly understand. If God is to be truly God, He must be beyond our complete understanding.

The doctrine of the Trinity is not merely a speculative doctrine. It is a doctrine of tremendous daily practical importance. It enters into the very foundation of our experience, if our experience is a truly Christian one. For example, in our prayers, we need God the Father, to whom we pray; we need God the Son, through whom we pray; and we need God the Holy Spirit, in whom we pray. Also, in our worship, we need God the Father, the very center of our worship; we need the Son, through whom we approach the Father in our worship; and we need the Holy Spirit, by whom we worship. But all three—Father, Son, and Holy Spirit—are the objects of our worship. The following doxology is thoroughly Christian in its worship:

---

* Unitarianism denies the Christian doctrine of the Trinity and instead teaches that God exists in only one person.

> Praise God from whom all blessings flow,
>> Praise Him all creatures here below.
> Praise Him above, ye heavenly hosts,
>> Praise Father, Son, and Holy Ghost.

So, also, is the Gloria Patri, the words of which we so often sing, but the thought of which we so seldom grasp: "Glory be to the Father and to the Son and to the Holy Ghost, as it was in the beginning, is now, and ever shall be, world without end. Amen."